The United States: Historical Atlases of the Growth of a New Nation ™

A HISTORICAL ATLAS OF Colonial America

Joan Axelrod-Contrada

The Rosen Publishing Group, Inc., New York

To my parents, my in-laws, and Aunty Delly for sharing their stories. Together, they've taught me that history is all about people.

Published in 2005 by The Rosen Publishing Group, Inc.
29 East 21st Street, New York, NY 10010

First Edition

Library of Congress Cataloging-in-Publication Data

Axelrod-Contrada, Joan.
A historical atlas of colonial America/by Joan Axelrod-Contrada.—1st ed.
p. cm.—(The United States: historical atlases of the growth of a new nation)
Includes bibliographical references and index.
Contents: The Age of Discovery—Spanish conquest—Other European claims—The thirteen colonies—Colonial life—England against France—The road to revolution.
ISBN 1-4042-0200-5
1. United States—History—Colonial period, ca. 1600–1775—Juvenile literature. 2. United States—History—Colonial period, ca. 1600–1775—Maps for children. [1. United States—History—Colonial period, ca. 1600–1775. 2. Atlases.]
I. Title. II. Series.

E188.A94 2004
911'.73—dc22

2003069313

Manufactured in the United States of America

On the cover: Top: An eighteenth-century etching by Paul Revere depicting the phases of the struggle of American colonists against the Stamp Act. Bottom: A nineteenth-century lithograph of Pocahontas protecting Captain John Smith from execution by Native Americans. Background: A map showing the thirteen original British colonies in the New World, originally published in *The Historical Atlas* by William R. Shepherd in 1923.

Contents

CANADA
LAKE SUPERIOR
LAKE MICHIGAN
LAKE HURON
LAKE ERIE
LAKE ONTARIO
Algomkins
Iroquois
Outowacs
Petunes destroy'd
The IROQUOIS or Six Nations
PENSILVANIA
MARYLAND
VIRGINIA
JERSEY
CAROLINA
Apalachy Mountains
Ohio or Bell River
St. Jerome or Oubach R.
Miamis or Twigtees
Here C. Washington engag'd ye French 1754
Fall of Niagara
Philadelphia
Baltimore
Chester
Newcastle
Williamsburg
Jamestown
Hampton
Fredericksburg
Chesapeak Bay
Delawar Bay
C. May
C. Charles
C. Henry
Currituk Inlet
Currituk Sound
Albemarl Sound
Cherakees
English Fort
40
45

INTRODUCTION

Few Europeans rushed to settle in North America, the New World "discovered" by Christopher Columbus in 1492. Most came only to search for a direct route to Asia, the mythical Northwest Passage. Others, like the Spanish conquistadors, came in search of gold. Rumors of gold sent explorers on expeditions throughout the American wilderness.

Spain was the first country to dominate the New World. In 1565, Spain established a settlement in Saint Augustine, Florida, now the oldest city in the United States. Before long, England challenged Spain for New World territory. In 1588, England fought off a possible invasion by Spain. This victory signaled the rise of England as a country with the power to establish colonies overseas.

The British colonies in America are shown on this eighteenth-century British map. The British had been trying to colonize North America since 1586, when the lost colony of Roanoke was established off the coast of what is now North Carolina. The British lagged behind the Spanish, the Portuguese, and the French in terms of New World territorial holdings, yet they also controlled colonies in Canada by 1775.

British authorities viewed America as a land that could profit England and relieve its economic pressures. English men and women who suffered from poverty or religious oppression in England could find a new life in America. America became a place to settle.

Founding successful English colonies, however, proved difficult. Sir Walter Raleigh sent groups of settlers to Roanoke Island off the coast of North Carolina in 1584 and 1587. The first group returned home and the second group disappeared. The lost colony of Roanoke remains one of America's mysteries.

Then, in 1607, England founded its first successful colony in Jamestown, Virginia. France, Holland, and Sweden had also established colonies in America, but they remained only sparsely populated. English settlements, however, attracted a huge population, and soon, a string of thirteen English colonies were established along the East Coast.

The English settlers pushed Native Americans off land they had occupied for thousands of years. Native Americans often developed alliances with the French who generally posed less of a threat to their way of life. English settlers wanted to expand their settlements farther into French and Indian lands to the west of the Appalachian Mountains.

War between the French and English became unavoidable. Spain stayed out of the conflict until 1762 when it joined France in its battle against the English. This choice ultimately cost Spain Florida, which went to the English. The English also won Canada from the French.

The French and Indian War (1754–1763) changed the relationship between the colonists and England. The war had been expensive. England wanted the colonists to pay some of the costs. The colonists rebelled against British taxes and British troops stationed in American cities. A new America had emerged. By 1775, it had become home for a people who fully considered themselves Americans.

CHAPTER ONE
The Age of Discovery

European explorers "discovered" North America by accident. Actually, European navigators were searching for a new sea route to Asia. Even when Christopher Columbus reached the Caribbean in 1492, he believed that he had reached the East Indies. This is why he called the people living on the Bahama Islands "Indians."

Long before Columbus's voyage, Italian merchants like Marco Polo had found spices and silks in Asia beginning in the 1200s. At the time, traders made the difficult overland journey from Europe to Asia in caravans. Bandits frequently robbed them of their goods.

If traders could get to Asia's profitable goods by traveling over water, all of the problems associated with land travel could be eliminated. Columbus figured that since the world was round, he could sail west from Europe and eventually reach Asia. But he had no idea that the continent of North America, a landmass completely unknown to Europeans, stood in his way. Finally, on October 12, 1492, after more than thirty days at sea, Columbus sighted land. He landed in the Bahamas on October 29, in an area he believed was the eastern part of Asia.

But it was only for Europeans that Columbus had discovered new lands. Native Americans had already been living in North America for thousands of years. For them, the arrival of Europeans sometimes resulted in friendship

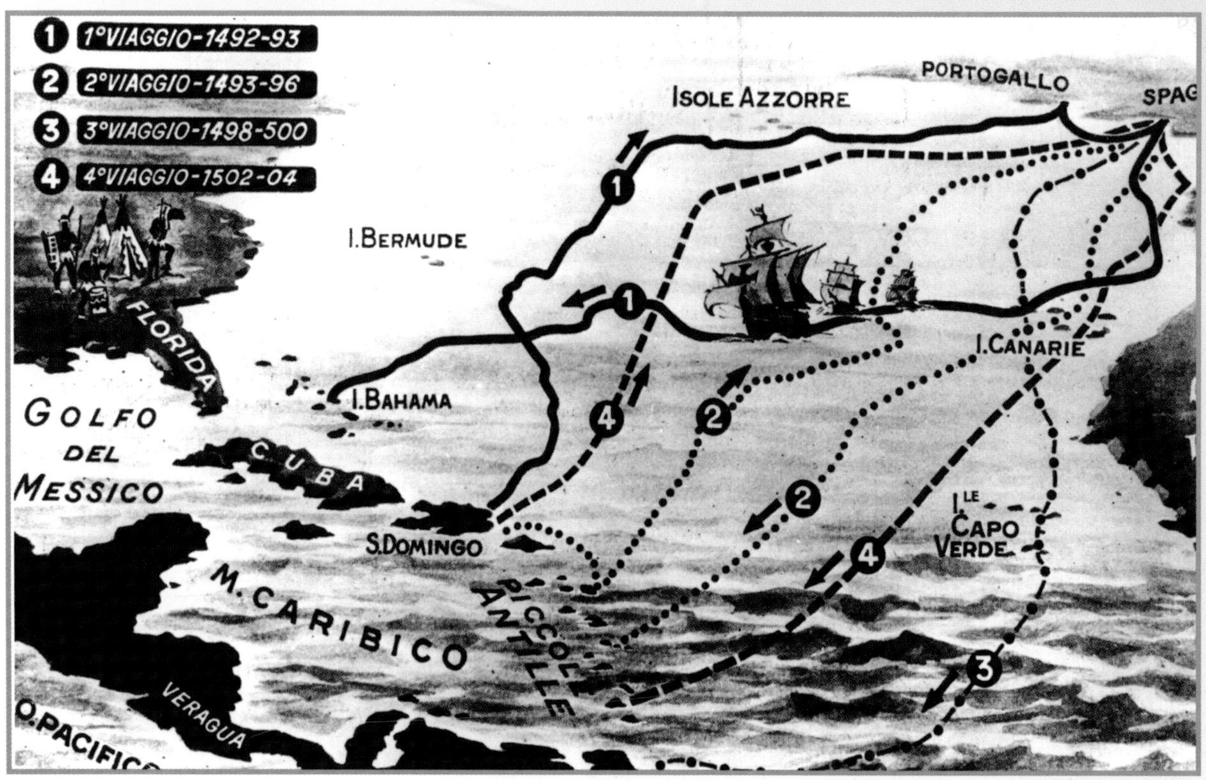

This Italian map illustrates the four voyages of Christopher Columbus (1451–1506) between 1492 and 1504. Searching for a western route to Asia, Columbus altered world history when he landed in the Caribbean in 1492. Columbus is credited with the discovery of America and for helping Spain colonize the New World. Today, opinions about Columbus are mixed. Although his discovery furthered European colonization and profits, the mixing of Native American and European cultures caused a massive depopulation of Indians due to widespread disease in the Americas.

and new goods. Ultimately, however, it translated into devastating human losses. Because Native Americans lacked resistance to European diseases such as smallpox and measles, hundreds of thousands of Indians died. Others were killed outright by the Europeans. To the Native Americans, the Europeans brought genocide and a complete disruption of their culture.

Native Americans

Between 20,000 and 30,000 years ago, long before Europeans colonized the Americas, ancient Indians traveled across Asia and into North America on a land bridge known as Beringia. This land bridge, once a giant glacier that has since melted, eventually became the strip of ocean known today as the Bering Strait. Scientists believe that hunters followed wild game across the 56-mile (90-kilometer) land belt leading from Russia to Alaska.

By the 1400s, about a million people lived in what are now the United States and Canada. Most Indians living in North America were nomadic hunters and gatherers. Some also settled and became farmers.

Groups in the same geographic regions tended to live similarly and spoke the same languages. Hundreds of smaller tribes lived within these different cultural groups, many harboring age-old rivalries with other tribes.

In the eastern woodlands, most tribes belonged to either the Algonquian or Iroquoian language group. The Algonquians had a bitter rivalry with the Iroquois. In what is now upstate New York, the Iroquois formed a league in which tribes agreed not to wage war against each other. Some historians believe the League of Five Nations, which was a democracy, was at least a partial model for the government of the United States.

In contrast, the Native Americans of the Southeast were settled farmers who grew a variety of crops, including tobacco, which had a bitter taste. Europeans, however, found a way to produce a sweeter

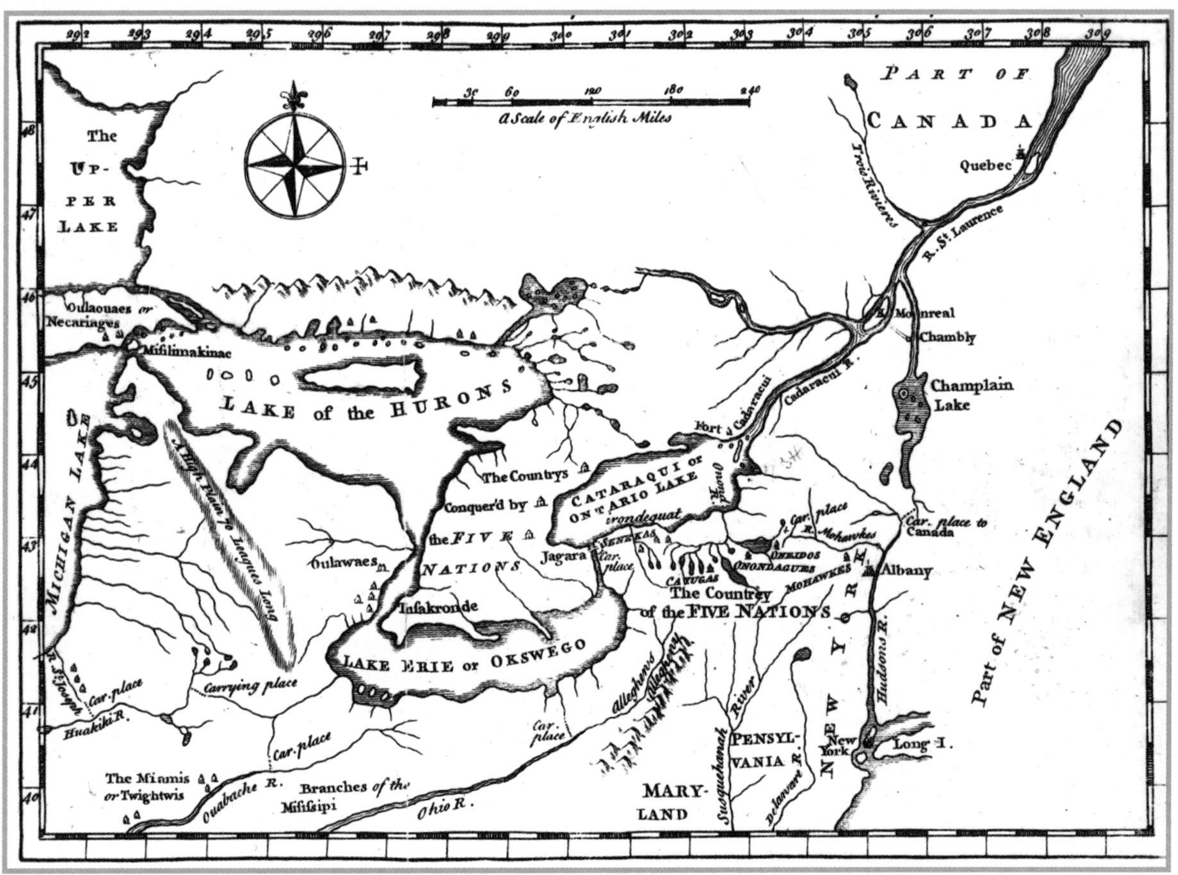

The country of Five Nations (present-day New York State and Canada) is seen on this map, created in 1650. The Five Nations were a confederation of five Indian tribes (the Mohawk, Oneida, Onondaga, Cayuga, and Seneca). Later in 1722, a sixth tribe (the Tuscarora) joined the group, which then became the Six Nations. Unified by a desire for peace and to prevent invasion from outside tribes, the Six Nations created a common council of fifty, known as sachems (chiefs). Sachems were responsible for making decisions and creating laws.

tobacco more to their liking in the warmer climate of the Southeast.

Meanwhile, in the arid Southwest, Native Americans were known as Pueblo Indians because they lived in multifamily units called *pueblos*. The Pueblo produced sophisticated pottery and textiles that they sometimes traded for meat. On the Great Plains, Indians trailed herds of buffalo all the way to the eastern coast of the continent.

The Italian explorer John Cabot (1450–1499) sailed from England in 1496 with permission from King Henry VII to "search for unknown lands." Although his first voyage failed (he had to return to England because of bad weather and inadequate provisions), his next voyage one year later proved successful. While historians disagree as to where Cabot made his North American landfall, like Columbus, Cabot mistakenly believed he had reached Asia.

European Inspiration

Columbus's voyage in 1492 inspired the European age of discovery. European kings increasingly sought the glory of claiming new lands. In 1493, Pope Alexander VI, who was a Spaniard, divided the New World (the Americas) between Spain (which got most of it) and Portugal. England and France, though, did not want to be left out of the competition. Both began sending explorers of their own to investigate the New World.

John Cabot

King Henry VII of England regretted missing out on Columbus's historic voyage because he hadn't wanted to finance the journey. When Italian explorer John Cabot offered to finance his own voyage to Asia, the frugal king quickly granted his approval. Cabot went in search of the Northwest Passage, a mythical shortened sea route leading through or around North America to the riches of Asia.

Commissioned by King Henry, Cabot sailed into the North Atlantic in May 1497. About one month later, he reached the coast of Newfoundland on the morning of June 24. (Historians disagree as to the precise location of Cabot's landfall, and some claim he actually landed on nearby

Cape Breton Island.) Cabot then turned south toward the land that is now Canada and claimed it for England. For the next two centuries, Cabot's voyage remained the basis for England's claim to North America.

Amerigo Vespucci

America was named after the Italian navigator Amerigo Vespucci who sailed to the New World in 1499, seven years after Columbus. America was named after Vespucci (and not Columbus) because a German mapmaker, Martin Waldseemüller, believed Vespucci was the first European to reach the New World. Vespucci recognized that America was an entirely new continent, not part of Asia as Columbus had believed.

Vespucci was born on March 9, 1454, in Florence, Italy, and studied navigation as a youth. In 1499, he

This early map of the Americas was created by Theodore de Bry and published in 1596. The engraving features the explorers Christopher Columbus, Amerigo Vespucci (1454–1521), Ferdinand Magellan (1480–1521), and Francisco Pizarro (1475–1541). They were all navigators who had made New World discoveries during the sixteenth century. De Bry was among the first to publish maps and books that featured unusual illustrations of the New World for a European audience.

participated in an expedition to South America. Then, between 1501 and 1504, Vespucci made two trips to the New World for Portugal. As part of his journeys, he developed a sophisticated way of determining longitude.

Vespucci also wrote a vivid account of his travels, which Waldseemüller read. In 1507, Waldseemüller decided to name the new lands "America" from *Americus*, which is Latin for Amerigo.

Juan Ponce de León

Unlike most explorers, Juan Ponce de León did not come to the New World in search of riches. Ponce de León began his life as an explorer when he accompanied Columbus on his second voyage to the New World. Enchanted with the idea of exploring new lands, he established a colony on Puerto Rico in 1508. It was in Puerto Rico that he first heard of a legendary natural spring that restored youth. In 1513, Ponce de León set out to find this fabled "fountain of youth." Instead, he discovered a land he called La Florida after the Spanish words for Easter, *Pascua florida*. Ponce de León claimed this new land for Spain. In 1521, he returned to Florida but soon died after being wounded by Native Americans.

Giovanni da Verrazano and Jacques Cartier

On January 17, 1524, Giovanni da Verrazano, an explorer from Venice, set sail on a voyage funded by French merchants who hoped Verrazano would find the Northwest Passage.

On March 1, Verrazano reached Cape Fear in what is now North Carolina. Then he headed north along the eastern coast to avoid the Spaniards. Verrazano anchored in the bay of New York near a site that is today named in his honor: the Verrazano Bridge. He explored New York Harbor and Narragansett Bay. Then he sailed up the coast, passing present-day Massachusetts, Long Island, Rhode Island, and Maine, before reaching Newfoundland and heading home. Although Verrazano had mapped much of the Northeast, he had failed to locate a route to Asia.

Later, in 1534, France sent Jacques Cartier to search for the elusive waterway. He is remembered for his discovery of the Saint Lawrence River. Cartier explored sections of present-day Canada. Seven years later, Cartier returned to the New World to establish a permanent colony in Canada that failed within a year.

CHAPTER TWO
Spanish Conquest

For much of the 1500s, Spanish explorers dominated North and South America. At the time, Spain was the most powerful country in Europe. Its overseas empire (New Spain), which initially stretched from the Caribbean into South, Central, and North America, was more than ten times the size of Spain itself.

Conquistadors set out to claim the treasures of the New World for themselves and the Spanish Crown. Early in the century, explorers such as Hernán Cortés and Francisco Pizarro claimed fabulous riches from the Aztec and Inca Empires of Mexico and Peru.

After the news spread in Spain of the fall of the Aztec Empire to Cortés in 1521, hundreds of would-be conquistadors made their way to the New World from Europe. The rumors about magnificent wealth charged their spirits. These conquistadors traveled with priests in order to convert Native Americans to Christianity, specifically Catholicism. They hoped to be appointed viceroys (governors) of the new Spanish provinces. Two powerful conquistadors, Hernando de Soto and Francisco Vásquez de Coronado, set out in search of gold in North America.

Hernando de Soto

Hernando de Soto led an elaborate expedition through the American Southeast between 1539 and 1542, after taking part in earlier journeys to the New World. Hungry for wealth, de Soto searched for treasure, following the advice of Native Americans who claimed that gold could be found throughout the Southwest. Instead of discovering precious metals, de Soto came upon the Mississippi River in present-day Tennessee, but he fell ill and died before completing his journey.

De Soto was born to a noble but poverty-stricken family in Barcarroto, Spain. In 1532, he joined Francisco Pizarro in his conquest of Peru. In 1536, he returned to Spain a rich man who sought his own New World colony. King Charles I authorized him to conquer and colonize the region that is now the southeastern United States.

The king helped de Soto recruit hundreds of gentlemen, carpenters, blacksmiths, and priests to start his colony. On May 30, 1539, de Soto's party of more than 600 men, 220 horses, a pack of dogs, and a herd of hogs landed in Florida. During the next four years, captured Indians told tales of the riches that awaited

The Spanish explorer Hernando de Soto (1500–1542) treks across America in search of treasure in this nineteenth-century painting by Frederic Remington. After a lifetime of successful exploration in what is now Central America, de Soto and his crew were relentlessly attacked by Indians while traveling through the southern United States. De Soto died before the end of his journey, in Louisiana, where his men submerged his body in the Mississippi River.

de Soto north of Florida. Based on this false information, de Soto's expedition wandered across about ten present-day states, including Georgia, Alabama, Mississippi, Arkansas, and Oklahoma. De Soto and his men crossed the Great Smoky Mountains and the Mississippi River in their fruitless quest for gold.

Along the way, they brutalized Native Americans. Indians were killed or captured and their villages were burned. Native Americans who were at first friendly quickly became hostile. The Creek tribes reacted to the violence by killing many of de Soto's soldiers.

On May 21, 1542, de Soto became ill and died. His soldiers submerged his body in the Mississippi River so the Native Americans would not know that the expedition now lacked a leader. De Soto's army reached New Spain the following year.

Francisco Vásquez de Coronado

In 1540, Francisco Vásquez de Coronado set off from what is now Mexico in search of the fabled Seven Cities of Gold. His journey led him through the American Southwest and into Kansas. Although he never found the legendary cities, he established Spain's claim to land that stretched from present-day California to Oklahoma.

Coronado recruited a force of about 300 Spanish soldiers, 6 Franciscan priests, 800 Mexican Indians, and about 1,500 horses and pack animals. Fray Marco (also known as Marco da Nizza, or Father Marco), a Franciscan priest who claimed he had seen a jewel-studded city known as Cíbola in what is now New Mexico, served as Coronado's guide. The party headed north from Mexico in July 1540, crossing the desert and mountains. Cíbola turned out to be a Zuni Indian village of pueblos. Coronado stormed it, killing hundreds and expelling the survivors, but he found no gold or silver—only food for his hungry crew.

Coronado decided to press on to recoup his investment. In New Mexico, his forces mistreated Native Americans and plundered their food. In response, the Indians rose up against the Spaniards. Coronado responded by ordering 100 warriors burned at the stake.

The Indians wanted to oust the Spaniards. In the winter of 1540–1541, one Indian concocted a story about a wealthy kingdom called Quivera (also spelled Quivira) to

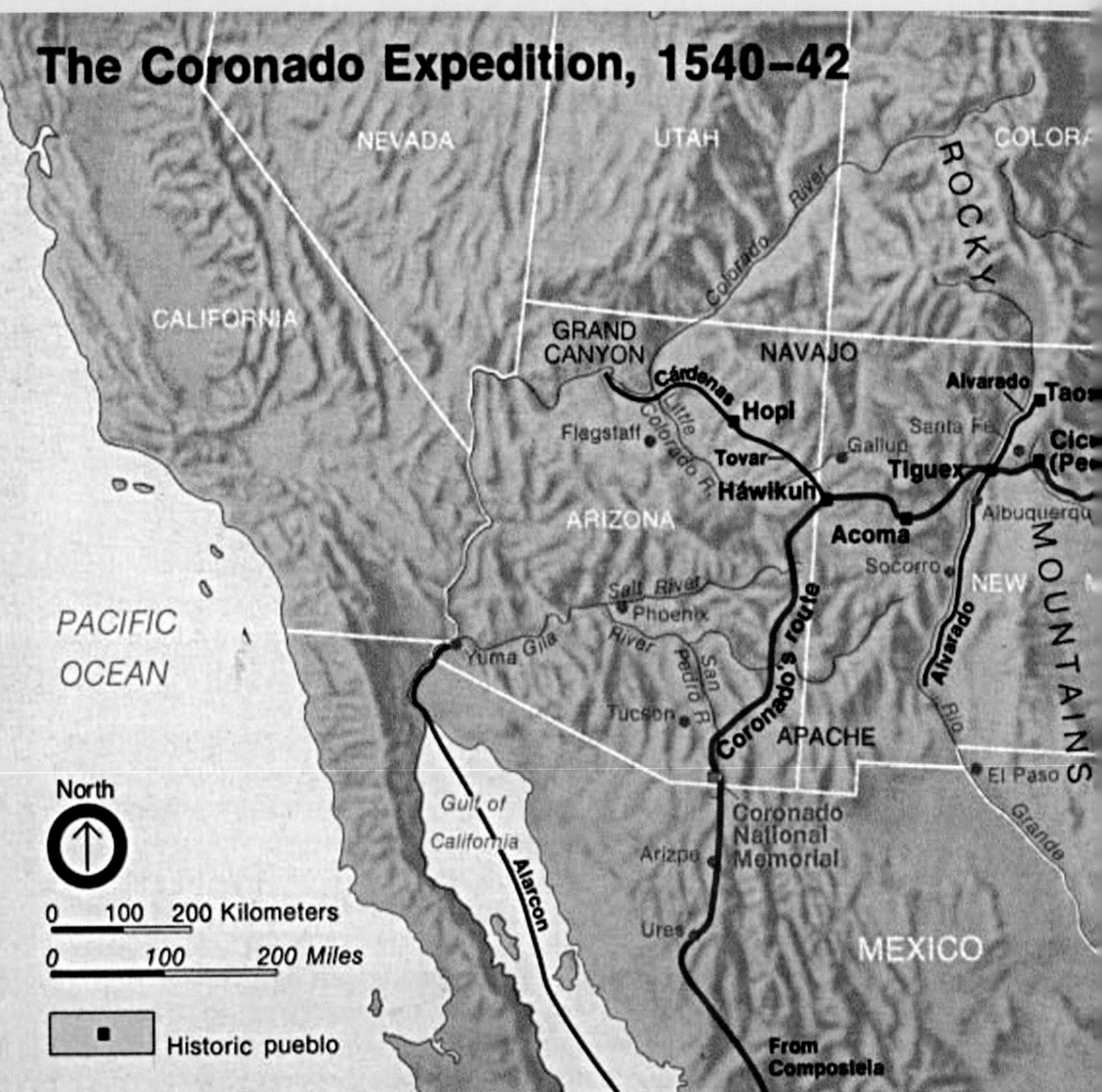

The trails of Francisco Vásquez de Coronado (1510-1554) and his expedition are shown on this map of the United States. Coronado and his men trekked through the American Southwest while searching for the Seven Cities of Gold. The fabled cities, which were actually Zuni pueblos in New Mexico, took Coronado on a journey over hundreds of miles. In the spring of 1541, the expedition split up. Coronado went in search of another rumored city of wealth known as Quivera, which also proved fruitless.

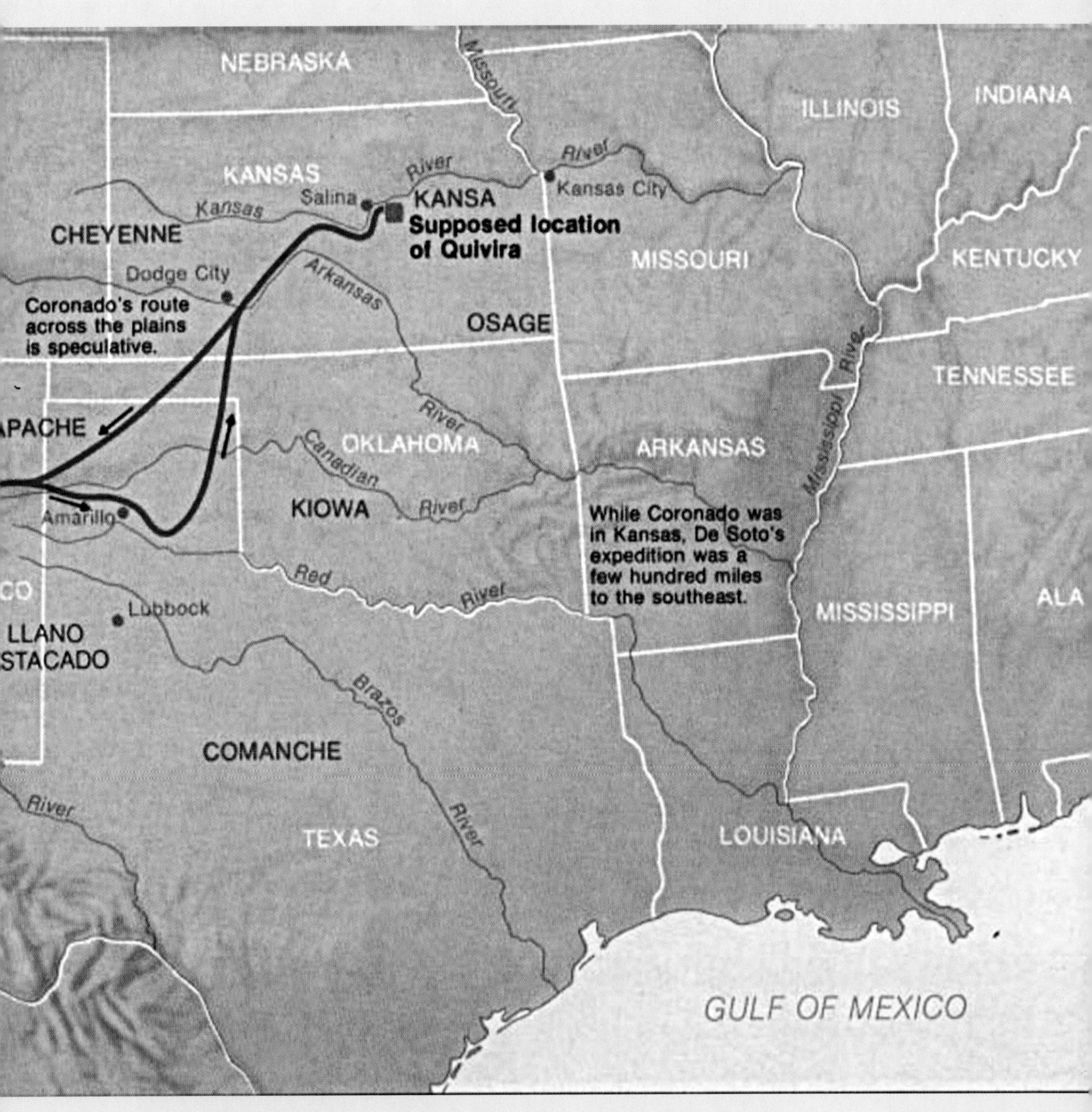
NEBRASKA
Missouri
ILLINOIS
INDIANA
KANSAS
River
Kansas
River
Salina
KANSA
Kansas City
Supposed location of Quivira
CHEYENNE
MISSOURI
KENTUCKY
Dodge City
Arkansas
Coronado's route across the plains is speculative.
OSAGE
River
TENNESSEE
APACHE
River
OKLAHOMA
ARKANSAS
Mississippi
Canadian
KIOWA
River
Amarillo
While Coronado was in Kansas, De Soto's expedition was a few hundred miles to the southeast.
Red
River
Lubbock
LLANO
STACADO
MISSISSIPPI
ALA
Brazos
COMANCHE
River
River
TEXAS
LOUISIANA
GULF OF MEXICO

the north. With this Indian as their guide, Coronado and his men crossed the Great Plains in search of Quivera, enduring weeks of hunger and thirst. They crossed present-day Texas, Oklahoma, and Kansas. Finally, the guide brought them to a modest Indian village of grass-thatched huts in what is now Kansas. This was Quivera. The guide confessed to misleading Coronado and his men so they might get lost and die. The furious Spaniards strangled the guide. Then they headed back to Mexico. In 1542, Coronado was prosecuted in Mexico for his abuse of the Pueblo Indians.

Spanish Settlements

The Spanish Crown was disappointed that America offered none of the riches of Mexico and Peru. Still, Spain wanted to keep other countries from claiming land in the New World. In 1565, the Spanish established a settlement in Florida named Saint Augustine. Today,

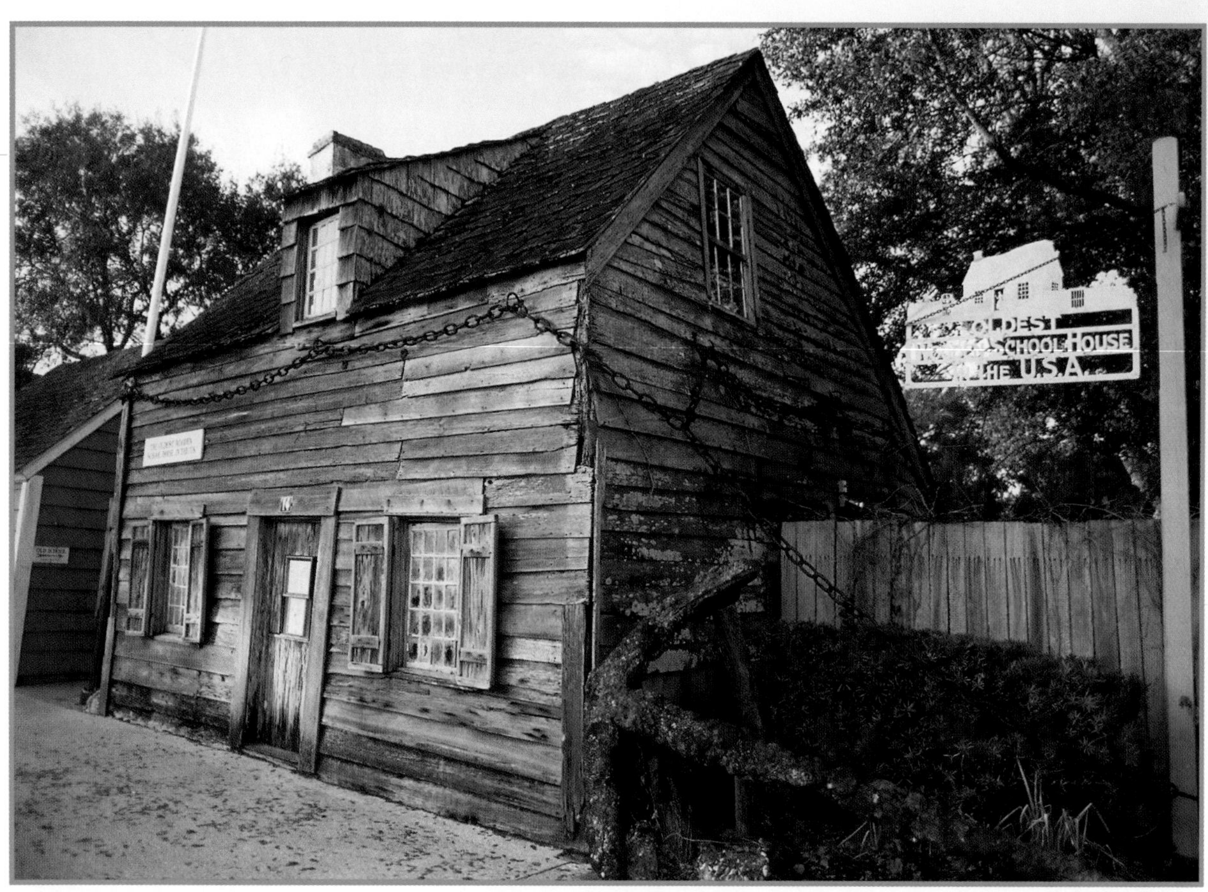

This wooden schoolhouse is among the oldest buildings in the United States. It is located in Saint Augustine, Florida, the site of one of the earliest Spanish settlements in the New World. Saint Augustine was established in 1565, forty-two years before British colonists formed the colony of Jamestown, Virginia.

Saint Augustine is the oldest city in the United States.

Spanish mariners, meanwhile, explored the lands along the Atlantic coast where the thirteen colonies would later be founded. Believing that the northern climate was too cool for tropical crops and too warm to sustain a successful fur trade, they decided the land to the north was of little value .

Only after French pirates began plundering Spanish ships in the Caribbean was Spain's interest in the northern lands reawakened. Then, in 1565, the Spanish learned that French Protestants—known as Huguenots—had built Fort Caroline in Florida. The Spanish Crown entrusted Pedro Menendez de Aviles to lead an expedition to seize the land from the French. On September 20, 1565, de Aviles and 500 soldiers led a surprise attack at dawn that killed most of the Huguenots at Fort Caroline. Within days, the remaining French in Florida surrendered to the Spanish.

After retaking Florida, the Spanish built forts as far north as present-day Virginia. But resistance by the Native Americans forced the Spaniards to retreat. Thereafter they decided that Florida adequately protected the Spanish Empire to the south in both Mexico and the Caribbean.

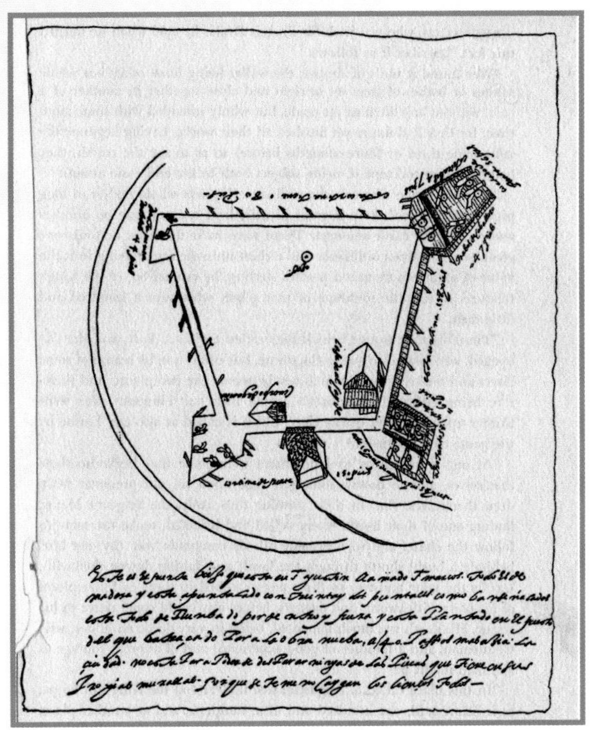

The Fort of Saint Augustine, shown in this diagram, was erected around 1566. Saint Augustine was raided many times by the British. Sir Francis Drake led attacks on the small settlement and burned it down in 1586. It remained under the control of the Spanish until 1763, when Florida was ceded to England. Florida became a state in 1845.

Then the Spaniards moved into the Southwest. They conquered the Pueblo Indians and established the province of New Mexico. Santa Fe was founded in 1609. Spain referred to its North American territories as "borderlands" because they protected its wealthier southern empire, which stretched from Mexico into South America.

Spanish viceroys led the government in the colonies. The Spanish colonies were supposed to produce only goods that Spain needed and, in return, provide financial

The crumbling walls of this Spanish mission are located in present-day New Mexico. This site, once known as the Mission of San Buenaventura, was founded by Franciscan monks in 1631 and is situated near the Pueblo de las Humanas ruins.

support for the Spanish Crown. They did this by purchasing everything they needed from Spain. This economic policy, known as mercantilism, considered it favorable if Spain exported more goods than it imported. Spain strictly enforced this policy. England had also developed a similar policy but did not yet enforce it.

The Spanish king and missionaries also believed that it was their sacred duty to convert the Indians to Catholicism. To do so, they established self-sufficient Indian settlements known as missions. Each mission included a church, a school, shops, farms, and livestock. Indians were not allowed to leave the missions, which taught the Spanish methods of building, farming, and worshiping.

Pueblo Revolt

Spanish government leaders, meanwhile, established farms and ranches in the colonies. Landowners forced the Indians to

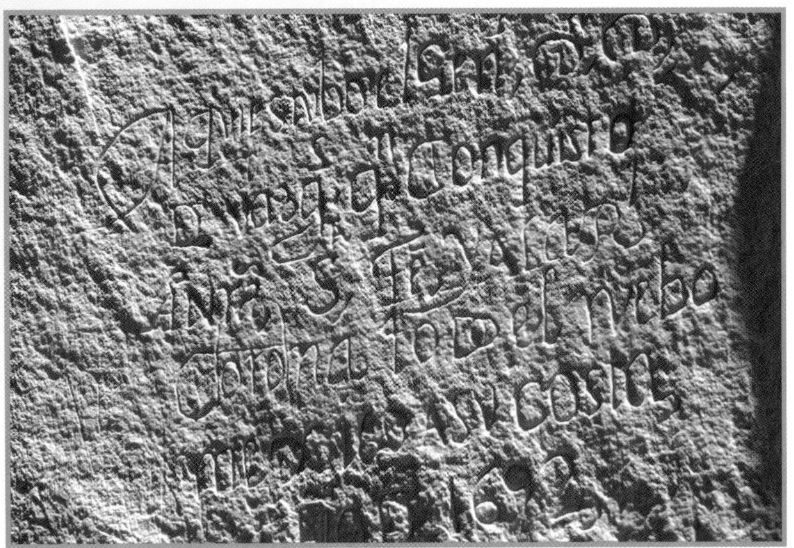

Frontier governor General Don Diego de Vargas carved his name in the sandstone of Inscription Rock at El Morro National Monument in New Mexico. It reads, "Here was the General Don Diego de Vargas, who conquered for our Holy Faith and for the Royal Crown, all of New Mexico at his own expense, year of 1692." Diego de Vargas recaptured New Mexico in 1692, when he led a Spanish army north from El Paso, Texas.

work on estates called *haciendas*. These landowners competed with the missionaries for Indian labor. As this rivalry increased, Spaniards became divided among themselves.

The Indians, in turn, became more unified in their opposition to unfair labor practices and bans on their religion. A long drought in the 1670s and 1680s created further hardships for Pueblo Indians who were at risk of dying from starvation.

In 1680, most of the 17,000 Pueblo attacked the Spaniards in a well-coordinated rebellion. They destroyed and plundered Spanish missions, farms, and ranches. The Indians drove the Spanish out of New Mexico.

A new Spanish viceroy, Don Diego de Vargas, recaptured the territory in 1692. The Spanish had learned their lesson: They never again outlawed the traditional religious practices of the Pueblo.

CHAPTER THREE
Other European Claims

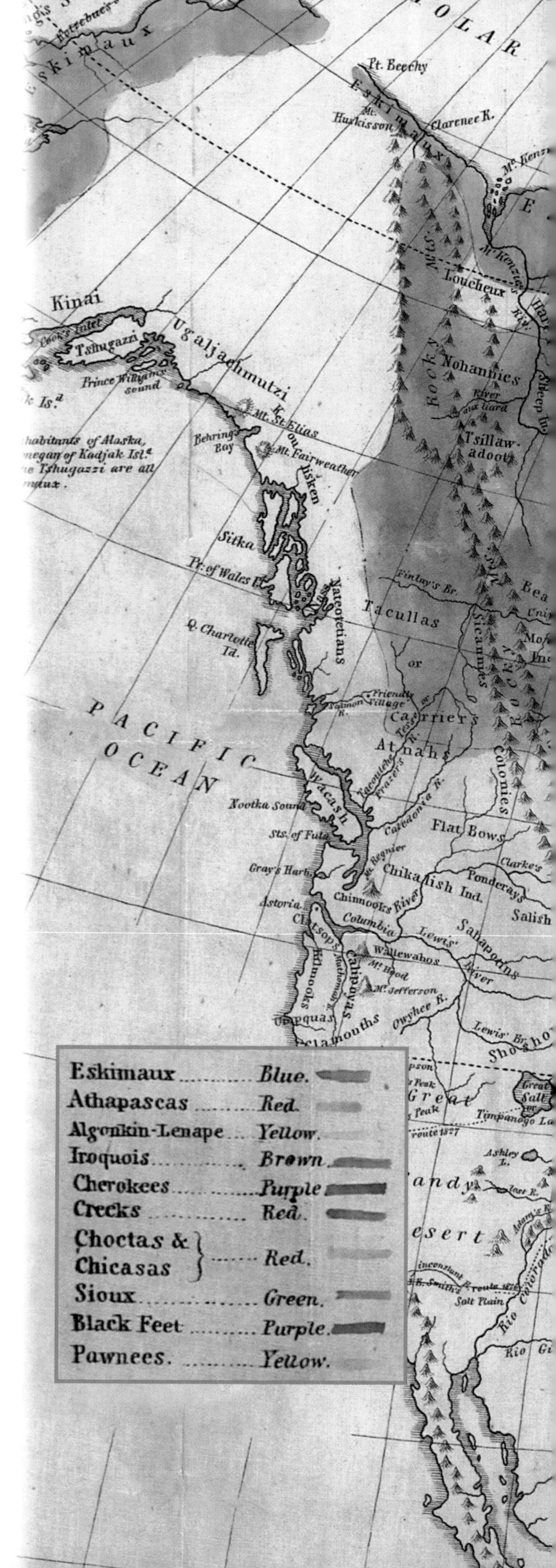

As the 1500s progressed, other European countries began to challenge Spain in the New World. They wanted a share of the riches. French, Dutch, and English vessels frequently raided Spanish ships for treasure.

But to have a steady and permanent share of the wealth, these other European countries needed to have their own foothold in the New World. Since the French Huguenots (Protestants) in Florida discovered that being too close to New Spain was dangerous, French and English adventurers became interested in the land north of New Spain. Because of its colder climate, Spain was less interested in this northern territory.

French and English frontiersmen began exploring the northern regions. They wished to find precious metals or a direct route to Asia, but they found neither gold nor the fabled waterway.

The lands of various Native American tribes are illustrated in this map of North America from about 1600. Drawn by Albert Gallatin and published by the American Antiquarian Society in 1836, it was designed to show the locations of Native American tribes and their linguistic heritage.

MAP
of the
Indian Tribes
of
NORTH AMERICA
about 1600 A.D.
along the Atlantic;
& about 1800 A.D.
westwardly.
Published by the Amer: Antiq: Soc:
From a drawing by Hon: A. Gallatin.
Pendleton's Lithography.
BAFFIN'S BAY
HUDSON'S BAY
James' Bay
Hudson's Sts.
Davis' Sts.
West Greenland
East Greenland
Eskimaux
LABRADOR
Sheshatapoosh
Scoffies
Papinachois
Montagneets
Micmacs
Etchemins
Abenakis
Gulf St. Lawrence
Nova Scotia
Chippeyans
Northern Indians
Algonkins
Chipewas
Sinibioins
Assiniboins
Tetons
Yanktons
Mandans
Minetare
Ricarees
Crows
Shyennes
Omahaws
Pawnees
Ottowas
Wyandotts
Five Nations
Menomenes
Winnebagoes
Potewatamis
Kikapoos
Miamis
Illinois
Piankishaws
Shawnees
Konzas
Osages
Padoucas
Panis
Caddos
Chicasas
Choctas
Cherokees
Muskogees
Creeks
Seminoles
Catawbas
Tuscaroras
Woccons
Delawares
Susquehannocks
Natchez
Attacapas
Adayes
Quapas
ATLANTIC
L. Superior
L. Michigan
L. Huron
L. Erie
L. Ontario
L. Winnipeg
Missouri R.
Mississippi R.
Ohio R.
Arkansa R.
Red River
Rio Norte
Rio Colorado
Canadian Fork
River Platte
Saskachawan
Fort Churchill
Chesterfield Inlet
Melville Peninsula
Athapasca Lake
Great Slave L.
C. Hatteras
Cape Cod

Instead, the explorers found an abundance of fish and small animals useful for trapping. It was then that they realized that a variety of animals could fortify a growing fur trade. Soon, the colonization of America would blossom. Europeans came overseas in the late 1500s and early 1600s. French missionaries set out to convert the Indians, the Dutch came to trade, and the English found a world of new beginnings in the American wilderness.

French Settlements

In 1608, Samuel de Champlain founded the first permanent French settlement (New France) in the New World. This settlement in Quebec, Canada, provided French explorers, fur trappers, missionaries, and settlers with a foundation from which they could move south into America. New France, however, remained sparsely populated since the French Crown allowed only French Roman Catholics into the colony.

Champlain made friends with the local Huron and Algonquian tribes. The French, armed with guns, supported the Algonquian in raids against the Iroquois. This alliance, however, made the Iroquois bitter enemies. It also inspired Native Americans to want guns, which made warfare between the groups deadlier.

Dutch and Swedish Settlements

In 1609, Englishman Henry Hudson set sail for the third time in the service of the Dutch. Hudson's goal was to find the elusive Northwest Passage to Asia. During the voyage, he sailed up the river that now bears his name. His enthusiastic report on the bounty of coastal New England brought Dutch traders to the scene within a few years. In 1626, the Dutch bought Manhattan Island

English navigator Henry Hudson (1565–1611) sailed three times in search of the Northwest Passage to Asia, exploring Arctic waters in the Canadian North and the Northeastern waters of the United States. On his third and final voyage mutineers set him adrift in a small boat along with a few of his shipmates. Hudson presumably froze to death in icy waters. The Hudson River was named in his honor.

from several Indian chiefs in exchange for tools such as axes, hoes, and drilling awls. The Dutch may have also offered the Indians wampum, which were beads made from shells that the Indians used as currency. In fact, wampum was an acceptable form of currency on Manhattan Island until 1701. Historians often claim the value of the exchange was about twenty-four dollars, then the equivalent of about sixty Dutch guilders. The Dutch called their settlement New Netherland. Swedes and Finns settled in a nearby area known as New Sweden, which was later absorbed by the Dutch. The Swedes, who farmed cold forests in their homeland, gave America the log cabin.

A miniature portrait of Queen Elizabeth I (1533–1603) is seen inside this jeweled enamel brooch from the late sixteenth century. Elizabeth I was one of England's most beloved monarchs, serving the country from 1559 to 1603. Her conservative leadership helped England become one of the world's most powerful nations.

English Settlements

Before England could become a major power in the New World, it needed to challenge Spain at home. Queen Elizabeth I believed that England's strength as a nation depended on her power at sea. She sent her "sea-dogs," a common term for English pirates, to raid the goods from Spanish ships. In 1587, Sir Francis Drake, one of the most famous of these pirates, burned a large part of the Spanish armada, or fleet.

In response, King Philip II of Spain invaded England. But the Spanish fleet proved less powerful than expected. In 1588, the British defeated the Spanish Armada. This event marked the decline of Spain and the rise of England.

The time was ripe for the English colonization of America. Writers

Settled areas before 1700 are approximated in this map of the area that would later become the United States after the American Revolution. The British colonists were confined to New England's thirteen colonies along the east coast. French settlements were established in the north and west, and Spanish settlements could be found in the south. The map key *(bottom right)* indicates colonial towns, forts, and missions, as well as native American villages.

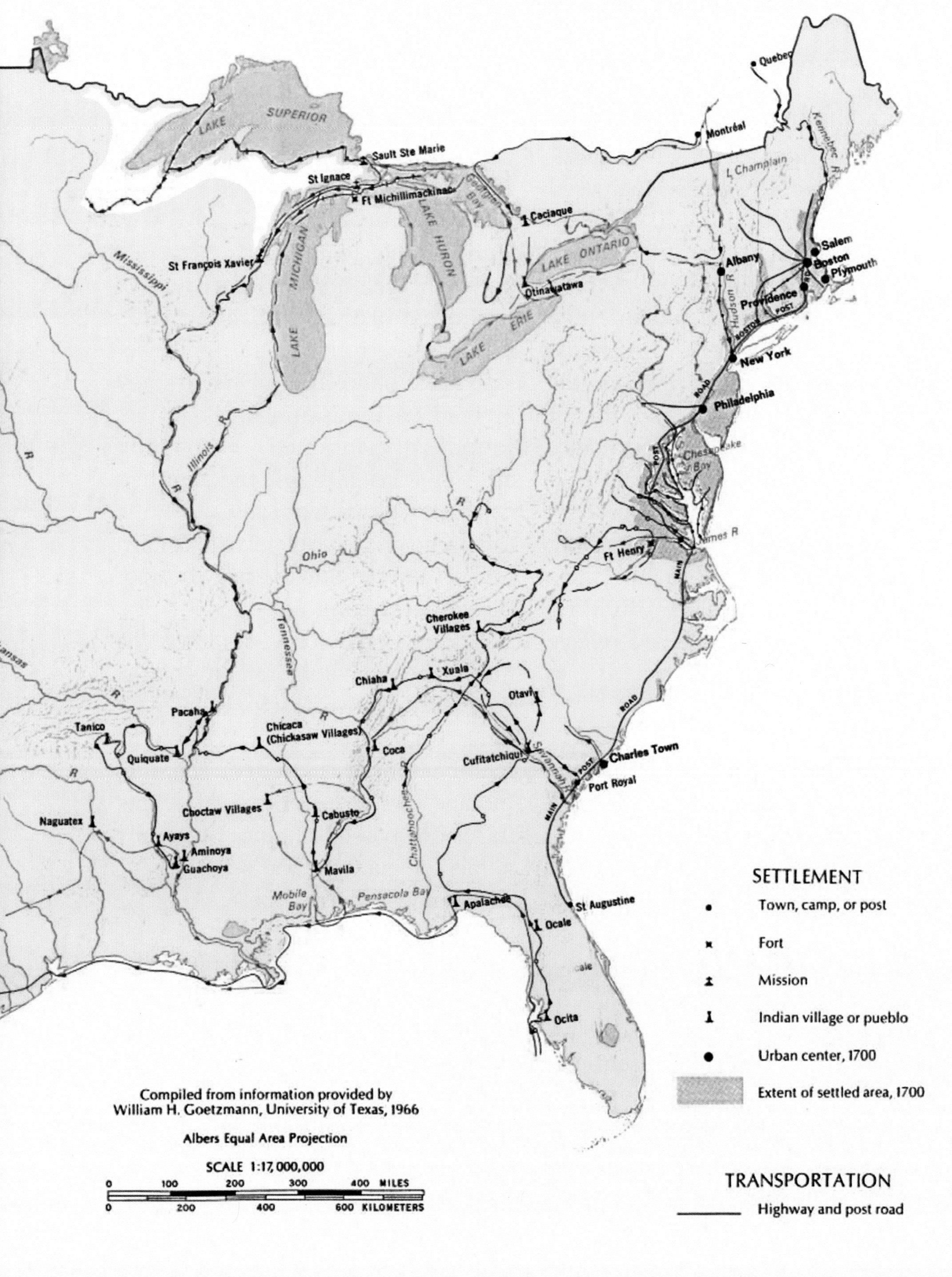
LAKE SUPERIOR
Sault Ste Marie
St Ignace
Ft Michillimackinac
Georgian Bay
LAKE MICHIGAN
LAKE HURON
LAKE ONTARIO
LAKE ERIE
Caciaque
Otinawatawa
St François Xavier
Mississippi
Illinois R
Ohio
Tennessee
Montréal
Quebec
L Champlain
Kennebec R
Albany
Hudson R
Salem
Boston
Plymouth
Providence
BOSTON POST RD
New York
Philadelphia
ROAD
POST
Chesapeake Bay
James R
Ft Henry
MAIN
Cherokee Villages
Xuala
Chiaha
Otavi
Chicaca (Chickasaw Villages)
Coca
Cufitatchiqui
Savannah
Charles Town
Port Royal
Pacaha
Tanico
Quiquate
Choctaw Villages
Cabusto
Naguatex
Ayays
Aminoya
Guachoya
Mavila
Mobile Bay
Pensacola Bay
Chattahoochee
Apalachee
St Augustine
Ocale
Ocita
SETTLEMENT
Town, camp, or post
Fort
Mission
Indian village or pueblo
Urban center, 1700
Extent of settled area, 1700
TRANSPORTATION
Highway and post road
Compiled from information provided by
William H. Goetzmann, University of Texas, 1966
Albers Equal Area Projection
SCALE 1:17,000,000
0 100 200 300 400 MILES
0 200 400 600 KILOMETERS

such as William Shakespeare inspired the English to be pioneers. Meanwhile, English trade grew. New industries such as the manufacture of wool had also increased England's wealth.

Prominent men persuaded Queen Elizabeth to plan New World colonies. These settlements, they argued, would extend England's trade to America and give jobs to the unemployed at home. The rise of sheep farming and the enclosure movement (laws that allowed landowners to fence off public lands) had forced many people off the land. These people flocked to England's already crowded cities. Building settlements overseas helped relieve economic pressure at home.

Roanoke

In 1584, Queen Elizabeth granted the right to start a settlement in America to Sir Walter Raleigh, an adventurer, navigator, and author. However, the queen would not permit Raleigh to leave her court to search for an adequate location for the colony. Explorers instead reported to Raleigh that Roanoke Island, situated off the coast of present-day North Carolina, was blessed with fertile land and friendly Indians.

Raleigh sent settlers to the island in 1585. This first group, however, suffered such hardships that they returned home. Two years later, in 1587, Raleigh sent another group of colonists to Roanoke, leaving them there while the ship returned to England for supplies.

The supply ships, however, were unable to return to America between 1588 and 1589 because of the threat of the Spanish Armada. In 1590, the relief ships finally set sail for Roanoke. But when they arrived on the island, the rescuers found it abandoned. Their only clue to the fate of the English colonists was the word CROATOAN, the name of a nearby island, carved into a tree. No one ever saw any of the settlers again.

Today, some 400 years later, the fate of the lost colony remains one of America's most fascinating mysteries. Could the settlers have become members of the tribe of Croatan Indians? Some historians think that this is one possibility since the family names of many of the settlers have survived within the tribe.

Other historians, however, believe that the settlers drowned at sea, were killed by Indians, or were scattered in different directions. In *Solving the Mystery of the Lost Colony*, author Lee Miller offers a new theory about the fate of the colonists. She believes that insiders within Queen Elizabeth's court possibly sabotaged Roanoke to discredit

Raleigh. Only time will tell which theory, if any, emerges as fact.

Virginia

Roanoke laid the groundwork for the first successful English colony in Virginia. This time, in 1607, English ships avoided the shallow waters around Roanoke. The first successful English settlement, Jamestown, was named after King James, who had succeeded Queen Elizabeth in 1603.

Jamestown nearly failed as Roanoke had. The land on which the settlement was built on the banks of the James River was swampy. English settlers had chosen the isolated site because they believed that it would be easy to defend against Indians. But the murky James River surrounding Jamestown bred mosquitoes, which carried malaria. The settlers drew water from the river to irrigate their crops and also for drinking. But since they also used the river to deposit their waste, drinking from the James River gave rise to diseases such as dysentery and typhoid fever. More than 6,000

The triangular Jamestown settlement is seen in this print as it probably appeared in 1607. Jamestown was the first long-standing British settlement in North America, named in honor of King James I of England. Jamestown barely survived as a settlement because it was built upon swampy marshlands near the James River in Virginia. Because its colonists relied upon the nearby river for depositing of waste and for drinking, many of its residents died from diseases such as typhoid fever, cholera, and malaria.

settlers died in Jamestown between 1607 and 1624.

Like the Spanish conquistadors, Jamestown's settlers preferred searching for gold to cultivating food, but the minerals they found proved worthless. Finally, Captain John Smith, head of the settlement, forced the colonists to work six hours a day in the fields. Then, in 1612, colonist John Rolfe learned to grow tobacco. Jamestown finally had a means of solid economic support. Rolfe also helped the colony by marrying the Indian princess Pocahontas in 1614. This celebrated marriage led to what became known as the Married Peace between the English and the Native Americans in Virginia. This period of peace ended, however, when Pocahontas's father, Chief Powhatan, died in 1618.

Pocahontas (1595–1617) protects English colonist Captain John Smith from injury by Native Americans in this lithograph from 1870. After saving Smith, Pocahontas visited Jamestown regularly, often bearing gifts of food. In 1613, Pocahontas was captured by the colonists, converted to Christianity, and baptized Lady Rebecca. Shortly after, she married colonist John Rolfe in 1614.

In 1619, Jamestown was allowed to create a more self-sustaining government. America's first legislative body consisted of a governor, his council, and twenty-two representatives.

Slavery

Virginia planters needed a sizeable work force in order to grow tobacco. At first, they relied mostly on white settlers who were indentured servants. An indentured servant was a person who had agreed to serve his or her master for a certain number of years. Once declared free, many indentured servants started their own farms. Therefore, the planters could not count on indentured servants as a permanent workforce. The planters needed to find other sources of manpower.

This painting by American artist Howard Pyle depicts the landing of a ship carrying African slaves to Jamestown in 1619. The British colonists were the first settlers in North America to grow tobacco. Because the demand for laborers became so great, a larger workforce was needed to maintain the fields. To remedy this problem, British colonists brought indentured servants and African slaves to the colonies.

In 1619, a Dutch ship transported twenty blacks from Africa to Jamestown. Historians believe these first blacks in Virginia started out as indentured servants. By 1640, however, the system had changed. The English took their inspiration from the Dutch, French, and Spanish who had regularly used slaves on their sugar plantations in the Caribbean. Plantation owners made the switch from hiring Africans as indentured servants to buying them as permanent slaves.

CHAPTER FOUR
The Thirteen Colonies

Success in Virginia inspired the creation of thirteen English colonies along the eastern seaboard between New France in the north and New Spain in the south. The thirteen colonies attracted far more settlers than earlier colonies had, partly because many Englishmen were unhappy in England. Land was scarce in England and poverty was common. Freedom of religion did not exist. America offered the best possibility of a better life.

English rulers also saw the benefits of colonization. America could provide another market for English trade and furnish supplies impossible to produce at home. After a truce with Spain in 1604, England could turn its attention to its American settlements.

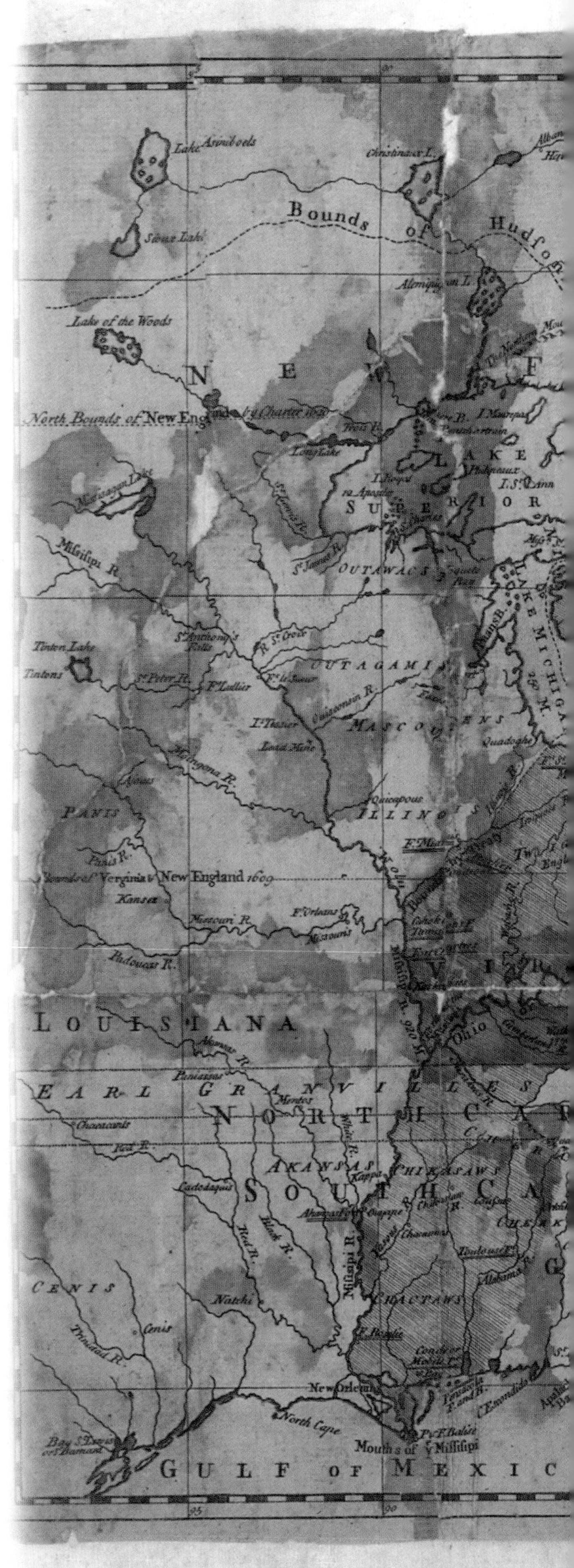

This eighteenth-century map illustrates both French and British settlements in North America around 1750. Although the two nations maintained diplomatic relations during the time of its creation, disagreements over North American territories soon sparked conflict in 1754. The French and Indian War (1754–1763, also known as the Seven Years' War) was fought between both nations in North America. In 1763, the British won the conflict, and settlements in the Treaty of Paris eliminated French claims in what would later become the United States.

A MAP of the BRITISH AND FRENCH SETTLEMENTS IN NORTH AMERICA
Explanation
The French Incroachments are shewn by Oblique Strokes, and their Forts with two Strokes, the English Forts by a single Stroke.
French Forts in Nova Scotia
Bay Verte, Beau-Sejour, two Forts on St. John's River, Canso.
New England
Richelieu, Cohasser.
New York
Sorel, Chambli, Crown-Point.
Pencilvania
du Quesne, with two Forts South E. of Lake Errié.
In the North of the Iroquois Coun.y
Frontenac, Toronto, Niagara, Pontchartrain, St. Ignace, St. Joseph.
Verginia
Sondoskie, Miamis, la Rocher, one Fort where Wabache & Ohio Rivers join, Chartres.
Georgia
Toulous, Mobile, Rosalie, New Orleans, Pensacola.
A Scale of English Miles.
Map Division
Library of Congress
80 Longitude W. from London.
75
70
65
60
55
Pt. of HUDSON's BAY
JAMES BAY
PART OF LABRADOR OR NEW BRITAIN
by the Treaty of Utrecht
CANADA OR NEW FRANCE
Mistassin Lake
Little Mistassins
Great Mistassins
Straits of Bell Isle
Cape Charles
Bell Isle
C. Hamilton
NEW FOUND LAND
GULF OF St. LAURENCE
R. St. LAURENCE
Anticosti
NOVA SCOTIA
Cape Britain or Isle Royal
Louisburg
St. Peters Bank
Great Fishing Bank of NEWFOUNDLAND
Placentia
Cape Race
St. Johns
Bay of Bulls
Conception B.
Trinity B.
C. Bonavista
Annapolis
Halifax
Fundy Bay
Fishing Banks of Nova Scotia
Sable I.
Browns Bank
Cape Sable
Quebec
Orleans I.
Trois Rivieres
F. Montreal
Iroquois
Messesagues
Nipisin Lake
Temiscaming Lake
St. Johns Lake
Saguenay
LAKE ONTARIO
Niagara
LAKE ERRIE
Forts
PENSILVANIA
Iroquois or Champlain L.
Crown Pt.
New Hamp Shire
Massachusets Bay
Boston
Providence
Connecticut
N. London
Cape Cod
Nantucket I.
Long I.
Staten I.
New York
Albany
Hudson R.
JERSEY
Delaware Bay
C. Henlopen
Chesapeak Bay
Williamsburg
Norfolk
Winchester
Alexandria
Fredericksburg
James R.
Albemarle Sound
C. Hatteras
C. Lookout
New Bern
CAROLINA
Catawbas
Brunswick
Cape Fear
Cape Carteret
Charles Town
Santee R.
St. Helena I.
Port Royal
Savannah
Fort Moore
GEORGIA
St. Simons
Fort William
Ft. St. George
Limits Stipulated 1738
St. Augustin F.
Pico lata F.
FLORIDA
Bounds of Carolina by Charter 1665
C. Canaveral
ATLANTIC OCEAN
Bermudas

Massachusetts

In the 1600s, a group in England known as Puritans set out to "purify" the Church of England. Some of these Puritans left England for Holland on a pilgrimage, or journey for religious freedom. These people became known as Pilgrims. The Pilgrims returned home from Holland so their children could speak English, but they remained unhappy due to their lack of religious freedom. Finally, on September 16, 1620, the Pilgrims set sail for America where they planned on settling in Virginia.

Their ship, the *Mayflower,* brought them to Massachusetts instead, where they started their own government. While on board the *Mayflower*, the passengers wrote and signed the famous Mayflower Compact, which determined their system of government.

That winter, the Pilgrims settled in the wilderness around what would become Plymouth. The weather was harsh, and they might have died of starvation if not for a friendly Indian named Squanto. Since an English sea captain had once kidnapped Squanto, he understood enough English to act as interpreter between the Pilgrims and the Native Americans. Squanto taught the settlers survival skills such as how to farm the land, catch fish, and trap beaver.

In 1630, another group of Puritans set out for America. This larger group held

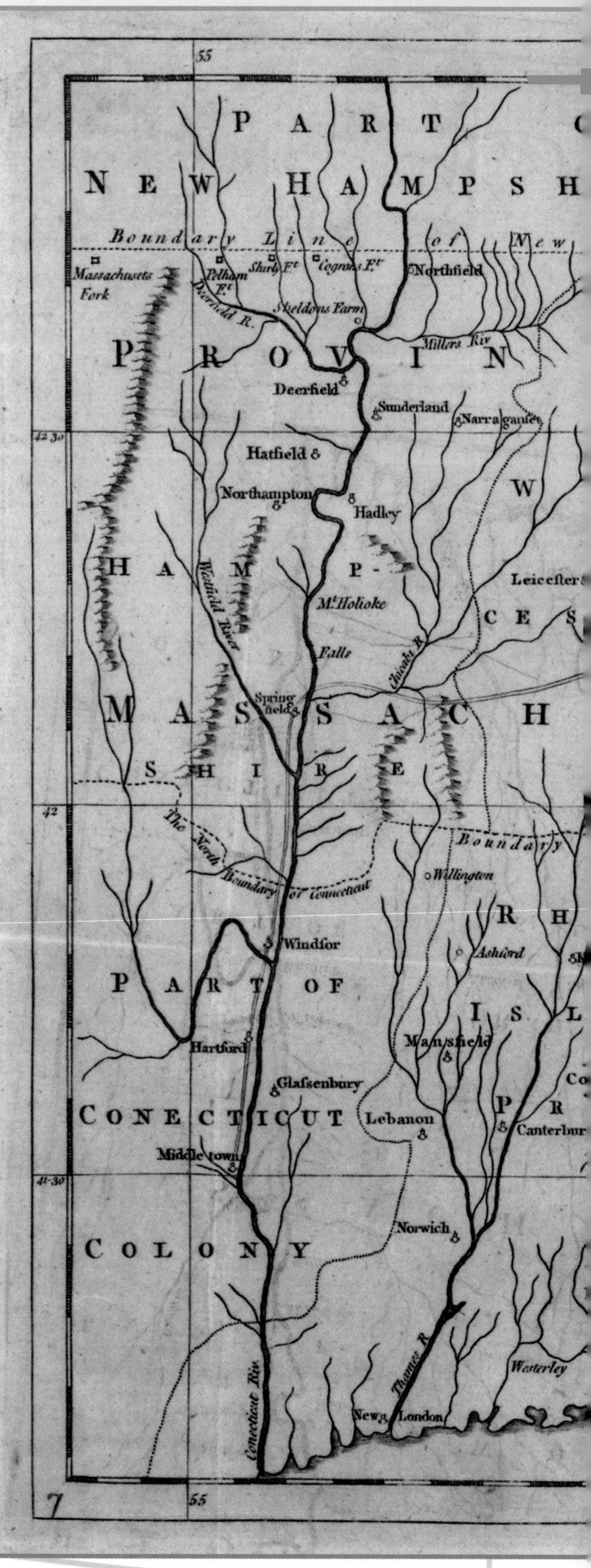

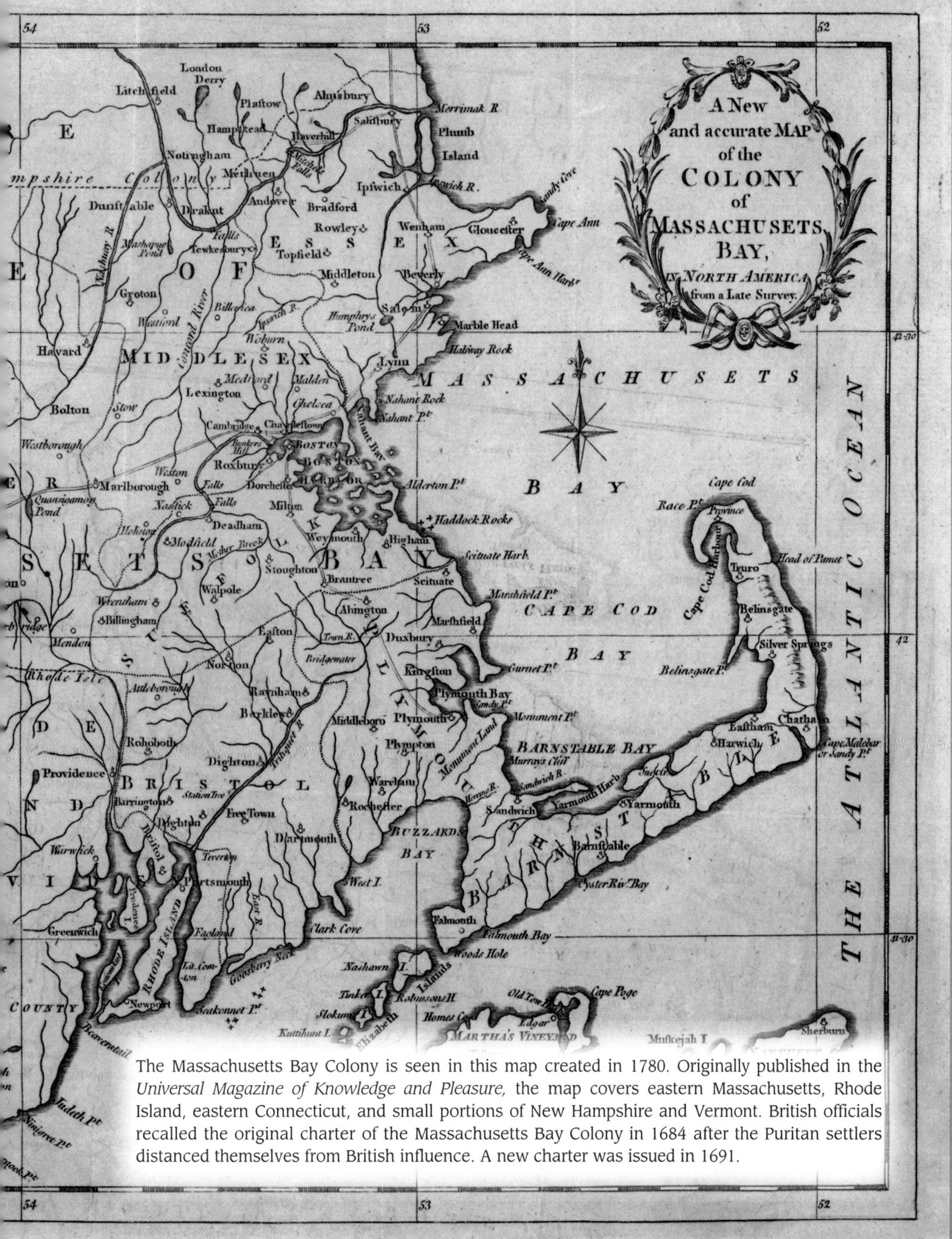

The Massachusetts Bay Colony is seen in this map created in 1780. Originally published in the *Universal Magazine of Knowledge and Pleasure,* the map covers eastern Massachusetts, Rhode Island, eastern Connecticut, and small portions of New Hampshire and Vermont. British officials recalled the original charter of the Massachusetts Bay Colony in 1684 after the Puritan settlers distanced themselves from British influence. A new charter was issued in 1691.

the charter to start the Massachusetts Bay Colony. They built the town of Boston in a harbor up the coast from Plymouth. Massachusetts Bay Colony grew quickly, partly because the company offered settlers free land. By 1640, Massachusetts had a number of new villages, including Salem, Marblehead, and Gloucester.

The somber-minded Puritans believed that idleness was a sin. They worked hard, clearing the land, catching fish, and building ships. Their settlements prospered. Native Americans, however, resented the growing presence of settlers on their land. In 1675, the Wampanoags, Nipmucks, and Narragansetts waged war on the residents of Plymouth. Metacomet, the Wampanoag leader known as King Philip, led the attacks. King Philip's War ended in 1676 after Philip was shot, and his corpse was quartered and beheaded.

The death of Wampanoag chief Metacomet (1638–1676) is depicted in this 1883 illustration from *Harper's Magazine*. After years of tolerating the colonists in Massachusetts, Metacomet rebelled against their continued encroachment upon Indian lands. In what became known as King Philip's War (he was called King Philip by the settlers), he destroyed several colonial settlements before being killed.

New England

In Massachusetts, the religious rules of the Puritans governed the lives of the colonists. These rules forbade such pastimes as dancing and playing cards, and settlers were required to attend church services on Sunday. Those who disagreed with the strict rules could leave Massachusetts and often did.

Some people headed west to the lush farmland of the Connecticut River valley. Those who thought the Puritans' ways were too strict settled around Hartford (present-day Connecticut) in 1635 or 1636. Another group thought the Puritans weren't strict enough. These people settled in New Haven (also in Connecticut) in 1638.

More colonists left Massachusetts after being banished for their religious beliefs. In 1636, the outcast minister Roger Williams founded

Salem Witchcraft

In the summer of 1692, witchcraft hysteria swept across the Massachusetts Bay Colony after a few teenage girls became mysteriously ill. Townspeople blamed their strange "fits" on spells cast by witches. Before long, more than a hundred people were accused of witchcraft. Fifty people "confessed," twenty-nine were found guilty, and nineteen were hanged. Finally, someone accused the governor's wife of being a witch. The legal authorities realized then that the witchcraft trials needed to stop. To this day, historians are not certain why the crisis occurred. Some scholars claim that the "fits" described by the girls were likely due to food poisoning or disease, while others claim that they were the activities of mischievous girls who felt repressed by Puritan culture. In any case, Salem remains a town known for its chilling past.

This seventeenth-century print depicts a woman who is using her "powers" to remove a book from the judge's bench during a trial in Salem, a town in the Massachusetts Bay Colony. Authorities finally put an end to the hysteria after the governor's wife was accused of witchcraft. Apparently, several young girls provoked the entire matter. They claimed they were possessed by the devil after hearing tales of witchcraft from a slave named Tituba.

Providence, Rhode Island, on land purchased from the Narragansett Indians. Two years later, Anne Hutchinson, who had preached to the women of Boston, joined other religious exiles in Rhode Island. Another group of colonists from Massachusetts moved north to New Hampshire for religious freedom.

Chesapeake Colonies

England's King Charles I gave George Calvert, Lord Baltimore, a grant to start a colony in North America that would welcome Catholics. Like Virginia, the colony, known as Maryland, developed a plantation economy based on the production of tobacco. Many poor Europeans came to America as indentured servants to work in the tobacco fields of both Maryland and Virginia.

In 1660, Charles II became king of England after a period of political upheaval, problems with Spain and France, and a civil war. His father, Charles I, had been beheaded for being a tyrant in 1649. Charles II rewarded some of the people who had helped him gain the throne by giving them permission to start colonies in America. These colonies became known as proprietary colonies because they were owned by individuals rather than by stock companies, charters, or the English Crown.

Charles II awarded New Netherland to his brother James, the Duke of York. In 1664, an English fleet invaded New Netherland. After the Dutch surrendered, the English renamed the colony New York. The Duke of York then gave the southern part of the colony to two English noblemen who founded New Jersey in 1664.

In 1681, King Charles II repaid another favor by granting William

King Charles II of England (1630–1685) is seen riding on a horse in this nineteenth-century engraving. He took the throne in 1660. Charles II led two wars against the Dutch, awarded British colonies in North America to his supporters, and tried to restore Catholicism as the religion of England. He is remembered for his selfish and flamboyant attitude and for being a patron of the arts.

Bacon's Rebellion

In 1676, Nathaniel Bacon led a rebellion of the common people against the privileged few who controlled legislation in Virginia. Although an aristocrat by birth (he was related to Sir Francis Bacon), Bacon voiced the concerns of many poor frontiersmen. Both Bacon and the frontiersmen felt that government officials had not responded forcefully enough to Indian raids. Bacon organized his own militia to attack Indians without government approval.

In the spring of 1676, Bacon was elected to the House of Burgesses. But when he attempted to take his seat, the governor had him arrested. Bacon gathered his supporters and marched on Jamestown. The protesters drove out the governor and set fire to the town. Bacon now controlled the colony. Then, in October 1676, Bacon died suddenly from malaria. Without his leadership, the rebellion collapsed.

Virginia colonists led by Nathaniel Bacon set fire to Jamestown in protest against Governor William Berkeley. They believed that the governor was not doing enough to protect them from Indian attacks. They formed a vigilante army to incite their cause. For many, their actions proved fatal: More than twenty of the colonists involved in the protest were hanged.

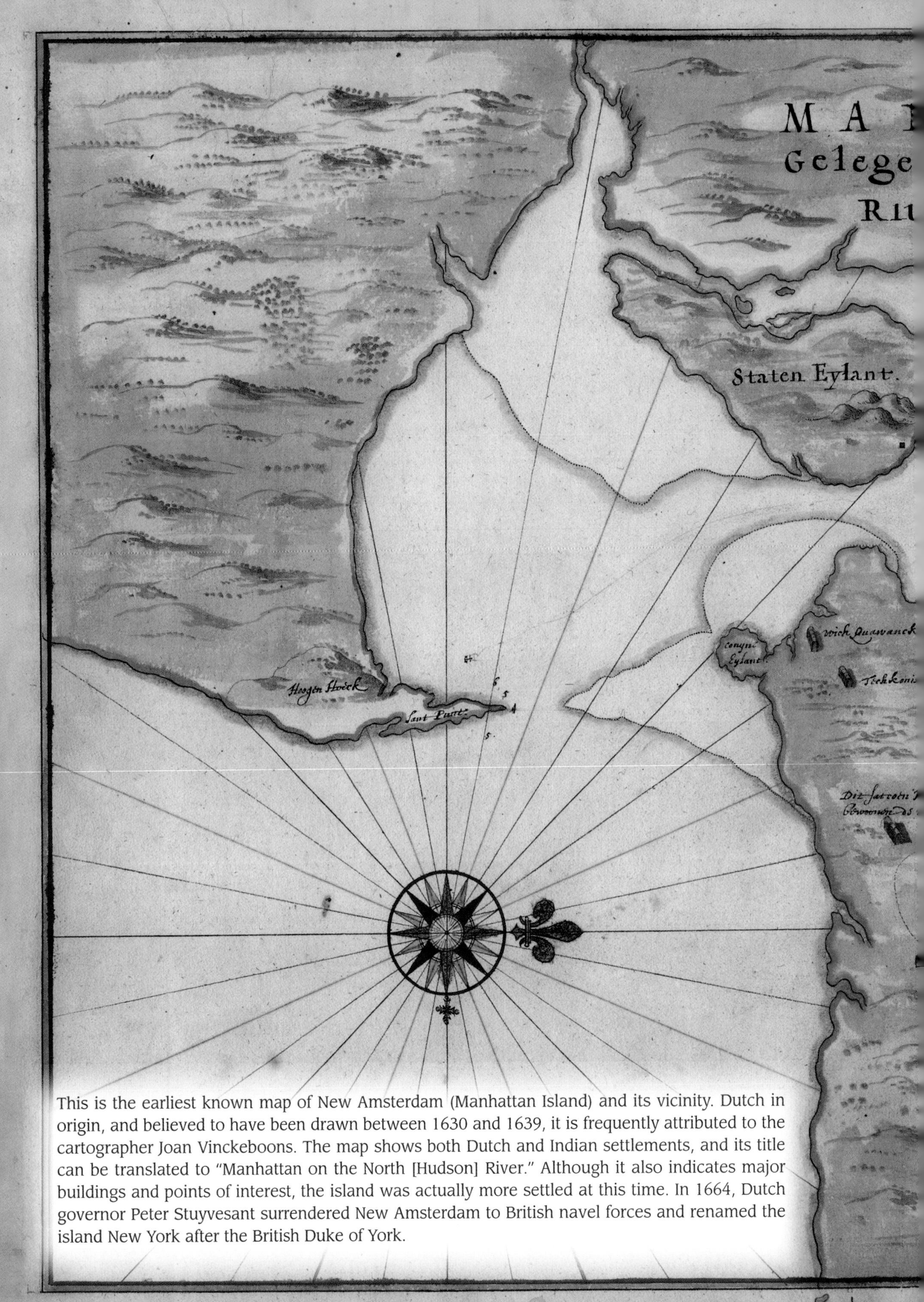

This is the earliest known map of New Amsterdam (Manhattan Island) and its vicinity. Dutch in origin, and believed to have been drawn between 1630 and 1639, it is frequently attributed to the cartographer Joan Vinckeboons. The map shows both Dutch and Indian settlements, and its title can be translated to "Manhattan on the North [Hudson] River." Although it also indicates major buildings and points of interest, the island was actually more settled at this time. In 1664, Dutch governor Peter Stuyvesant surrendered New Amsterdam to British navel forces and renamed the island New York after the British Duke of York.

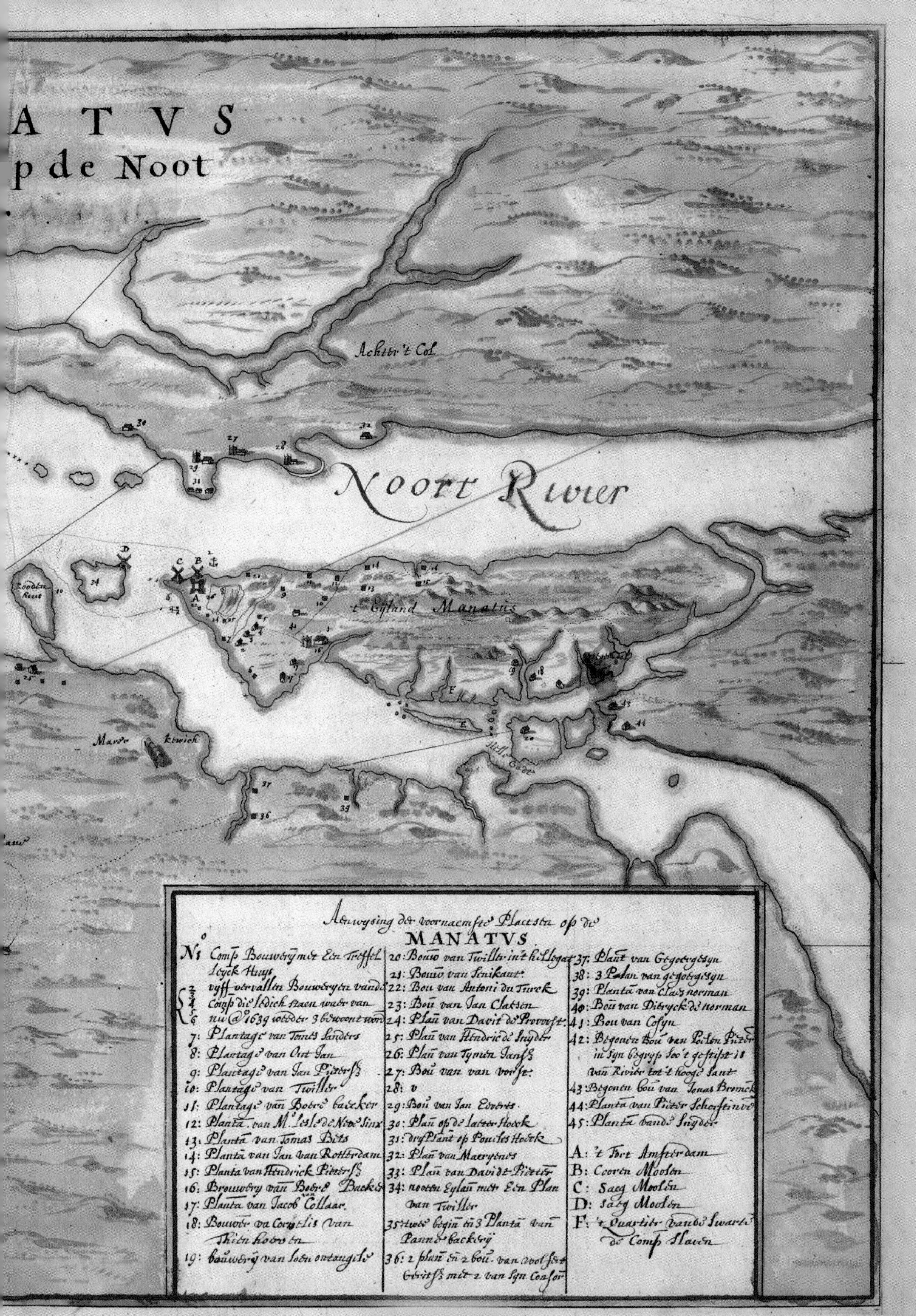
ATVS
p de Noot
Achter 't Col
Noort Rivier
't Eyland Manatus
Hell Gadt
Aenwysing der voornaemste Plaetsen op de
MANATVS
No 1 Comp Bouwery met Een treffelycke Huys
2 3 4 5 6 vyff vervallen Bouweryen vande Comp die ledich staen waer van nu ao 1639 iedder 3 bewoont word
7: Plantage van Tomes Sanders
8: Plantage van Out Jan
9: Plantage van Jan Pietersz
10: Plantage van Twiller
11: Plantage van Bor backer
12: Planta. van Mr. Isle de Nove Sinx
13: Planta van Tomas Bets
14: Planta van Jan van Rotterdam
15: Planta van Hendrick Pietersz
16: Brouwery van Bor Backer
17: Planta van Jacob van Collaar.
18: Bouwer va Cornelis van Thienhoven
19: bouwery van Joen ontangele
20: Bouw van Twiller int hellegat
21: Bouw van Senikant
22: Bou van Antoni du Turck
23: Bou van Jan Claesen
24: Plan van David de Provost
25: Plan van Hendric de Snyder
26: Plan van Tymen Jansz
27: Bou van van vorst.
28: v
29: Bou van Jan Everts.
30: Plan op de latter Hoeck
31: dry Plant op Poulus Hoeck
32: Plan van Maerytens
33: Plan van David de Pieter
34: nooten Eylan met Een Plan van Twiller
35: twee begin en 3 Planta van Panne backery
36: 2 plan en 2 bou. van wolfert Gerritsz met 2 van syn Consor
37: Plant van Gegorgesyn
38: 3 Plan van gegorgesyn
39: Planta van Claes norman
40: Bou van Ditryck de norman
41: Bou van Cosyn
42: Begonen Bou van Poulus Pieter in syn begryp soo 't gestipt is van Rivier tot 't hooge sant
43: Begonen bou van Jonas Bronck
44: Planta van Pieter Schorstinveger
45: Planta vande Snyder
A: 't Fort Amsterdam
B: Cooren Moolen
C: Saeg Moolen
D: Saeg Moolen
F: 't Quartier vande Swarte de Comp Slaven

Penn the colony of Pennsylvania, Penn's Woods. Penn was a member of the Society of Friends, or Quakers, a religious group that had been oppressed in England. Under Penn, Pennsylvania offered religious freedom. Pennsylvania's population grew. Other people in an area formally known as New Sweden split off to form Delaware in 1704.

James Oglethorpe (1696–1785), a British soldier and founder of the colony of Georgia, is depicted in this monument located in Savannah. Due to his work with prisoners in England, Oglethorpe believed in the idea of a British colony for the poor. He and a group of settlers departed from England in 1732 to begin a new life in Savannah.

Carolina and Georgia

As Virginia and Maryland prospered, Charles II gave land grants for two new colonies in the South: Carolina and Georgia. The eight English noblemen who founded Carolina in 1663 had trouble attracting settlers because of the earlier failure of Roanoke. In order to gather support, the owners offered settlers free land and religious freedom. Settlers arrived, as did black slaves brought over to work in Carolina's rice plantations. In 1712, the northern part of the colony split off to become North Carolina.

Georgia, created in 1732, was the last of the thirteen colonies to be founded. James Oglethorpe and his friends wanted to create a "charity" colony for poor people and debtors. These people would not be allowed to govern themselves, and the owners of the colony would instead make the decisions.

CHAPTER FIVE
Colonial Life

In the 1600s and 1700s, the population of the English colonies grew. At first, famine, disease, and hostile Indians slowed settlements in Jamestown and Plymouth. But in the mid-1600s, the great Puritan migration brought an increase of settlers. By the 1700s, immigration and a high birth rate created America's first population explosion.

Immigrants came from all over Europe. The population also grew because there were more births than deaths. Colonial settlers had increasingly large families because of surplus food. People grew healthier and lived longer. While the European population soared in America, the number of Native Americans dwindled. The Indians were dying as a result of both warfare and disease.

Indentured Servants and Slaves

Many Europeans paid for the cost of their journey to America by becoming indentured servants, but some indentured servants came to the colonies unwittingly. Kidnappers seized poor people, both children and adults, and made a profit by selling them. Some criminals were also transported to America as indentured servants. As soon as those indentured had worked off the terms of their labor, they were freed.

Others were less fortunate. Some Africans and Native Americans became slaves for life. Increasingly, plantations turned to slaves for their labor needs. Although some attempted to escape, fewer African slaves than Native Americans were runaways because they were unfamiliar with the American wilderness.

The Colonial Economy

As the population in the colonies grew during the 1700s, the economy stabilized. More people living in the colonies meant that more goods were needed there. This demand for goods led to increased manufacturing and trading within the colonies. By the late 1760s, 54 percent of the ships departing from Boston Harbor had port destinations along America's East Coast, not in Europe. These ships sold goods at colonial ports. They also distributed goods throughout the colonies that had previously been imported from England.

Plantations dotted the southern colonies. In Maryland and Virginia, planters grew tobacco. In Georgia and the Carolinas, they grew rice and indigo, a blue dye. A percentage

Slaves and indentured servants pick tobacco leaves and operate machinery at a tobacco factory in North America in this engraving from 1750. By the middle of the eighteenth century, the Southern economy was already dependent on slave labor. At that time, African Americans were closely associated with tobacco and its production.

Stono Rebellion

On September 9, 1739, slaves along the Stono River in South Carolina rebelled. The conflict began when about twenty slaves stole guns and gunpowder from a store and killed two storekeepers. Then they headed south toward Spanish Florida, to Gracia Real de Santa Teresa de Mose, a refuge that welcomed runaway slaves. Along the way, they recruited about eighty others to join their cause. Together the group burned seven plantations and killed twenty whites. Within a week, white militiamen put down the rebellion, killing most of the runaway slaves. Later, those who remained were captured and killed for their crimes. Although the South Carolina militia put down the rebellion quickly, others would follow.

of these products was then exported to England and the rest of Europe. The ships that carried tobacco to England returned with supplies for colonial planters. Over time, the colonies developed a regional economy. Each region (New England, the Middle Colonies, the Chesapeake, and the Lower South) formed its own economy based on the specific goods it imported and exported.

Regional Economies

In New England (Massachusetts, Connecticut, New Hampshire, and Rhode Island), settlers mainly grew crops for their own use. The rocky soil and harsh winters limited agriculture in the North. Besides, New England's shortage of navigable rivers made exporting and importing goods difficult and expensive. Because of this need for independence, New Englanders became self-sufficient. They developed communities with common areas much like English farms. Instead of using additional farmland for cattle grazing, all could graze their cows on the common.

Instead of earning a living by exporting agricultural goods, colonists became fishermen and turned to the sea for their wealth. They also built their own ships. These independent activities concerned the English, who wanted to control colonial trade.

The Middle Colonies (Pennsylvania, New York, and New Jersey) grew grain crops. The bread colonies, as they became known, lent themselves to the cultivation of wheat. Farmers sold their wheat in Philadelphia and New York and soon created the most successful economy of all the English colonies. On average, farms in this region produced about 60 percent more than they needed to survive.

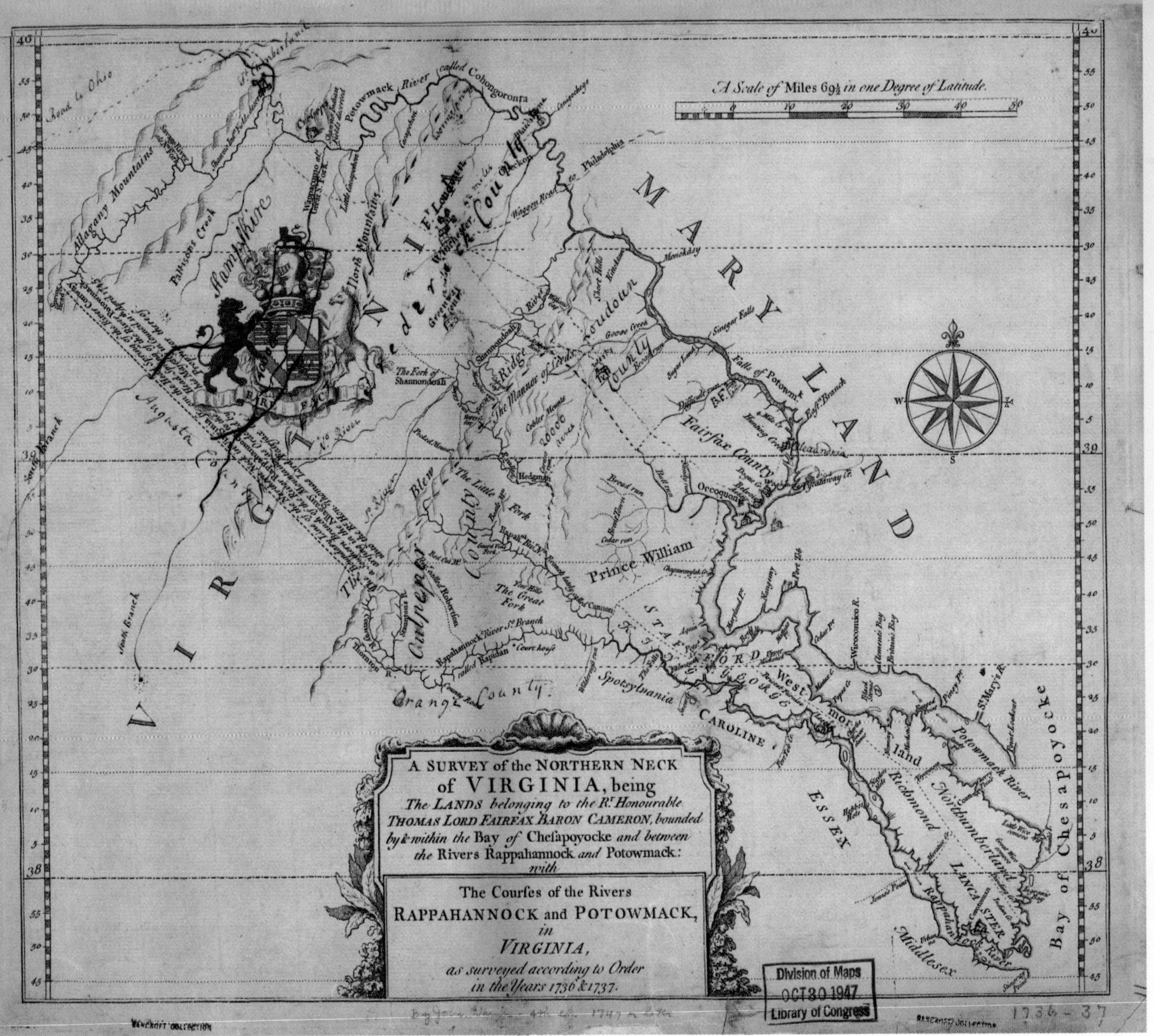

During the seventeenth century, many southern entrepreneurs owned large areas of land, such as this parcel in northern Virginia owned by Thomas Fairfax. This map, created in 1747, surveyed his land, which was bounded by the Chesapeake Bay and the Potomac River.

While wheat was a staple product of the Middle Colonies, the main crop in the Chesapeake Colonies (Delaware, Virginia, and Maryland) was tobacco. At the time, the profits from grain sales were increasing faster than tobacco sales. Because of this increase in profit, many tobacco farmers began converting their farms to produce wheat. Still, tobacco was the largest single export of the colonies, and the price of tobacco continually rose throughout the 1700s.

Plantation farming and slave labor supported the economy of the Lower South (North and South Carolina and Georgia). Southern crops included indigo and rice, a grain that was in high demand in Europe. Because of this demand, southern plantation farmers grew wealthy until conflicts between England and France caused a disruption in trade. Afterward, rice prices dropped and the South suffered an economic depression.

Simple Lives

Every member of a colonial family had work to do. Children worked either as indentured servants or on the farm. Women churned butter, sewed clothes, and bore children, all the while helping their husbands.

Some colonists in the 1700s made a living as artisans. Paul Revere, for instance, made a name for himself as a silversmith. Most colonists, however, could not afford to buy fine furniture or silver. They made whatever they needed themselves. Fireside crafts like quilting and needlework flourished. Girls received little education and were expected to stay at home.

Boys, on the other hand, were educated. Harvard College (later Harvard University), the first institution of higher learning in America, was founded in 1636 to train boys for the ministry. Soon America had many institutions of higher learning, including Yale, William and Mary, Dartmouth, Princeton, King's College (later known as Columbia University), and the University of Pennsylvania.

The Great Awakening

Because many colonists lived great distances from a church, religious participation suffered. During the 1730s and 1740s, a new breed of minister brought religion directly to the people.

The cold, rational religion of the mind gave way to a new spirit based on emotion. Sinners could be "saved." Anyone could be a Christian. Prayer meetings were filled with shrieks, shakes, and swoons. A religious revival was underway.

Charismatic ministers like Jonathan Edwards and George Whitefield brought the word of God to the American frontier. Known as the Great Awakening, traveling ministers brought a new sense of unity to Americans whether they lived in the north, south, or middle colonies.

CHAPTER SIX
England Against France

In the early days of the colonies, the French and the British lived in peace, separated by miles of wilderness. But as the colonies grew, they no longer wanted to confine themselves to the narrow strip of land along the Atlantic Ocean. English trappers and land speculators began heading west across the Appalachian Mountains. Traders from Pennsylvania cut into New France's valuable fur trade with the Indians.

New France was ready to fight to maintain its lucrative fur trade. But the English believed they also had a right to the land. Both France and Britain claimed the Ohio River Valley just past the Appalachian Mountains in western Pennsylvania as their own. Only war would resolve the conflicts stemming from these overlapping land claims.

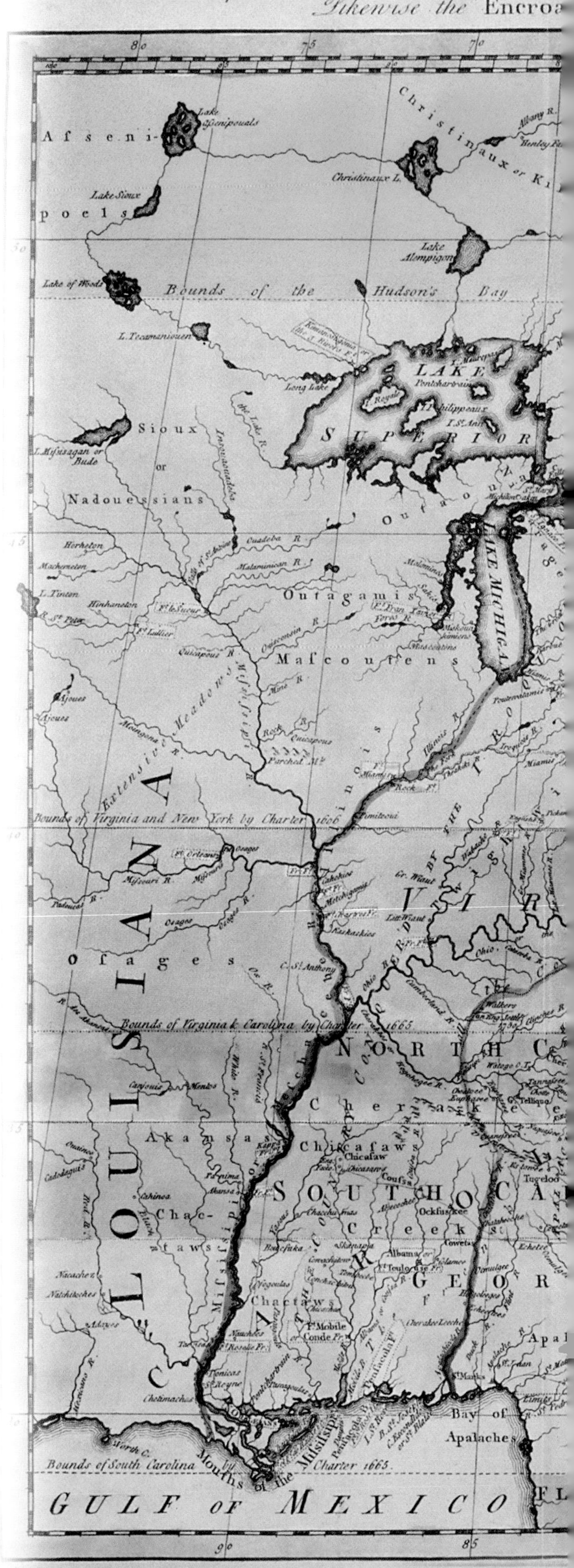

This eighteenth-century British map of English colonies in North America also features French settlements, depicted as "encroachments" on British soil. The map was created in 1755, just after the start of the Seven Years' War (known as the French and Indian War in North America, 1754–1763). After years of fighting, France gave up all of its major mainland holdings in North America to the British. This agreement was finalized in the Treaty of Paris (1763).

ts of the FRENCH, with the several Forts they have unjustly erected therein.
Longitude West from 35 Ferro
Longitude West from London
LABRADOR or Little Esquimaux
NEW BRITAIN
HUDSON'S BAY
CANADA
NEW FOUND LAND
GULF of St. LAURENCE
NOVA SCOTIA
LAKE ONTARIO
LAKE ERIE
PENSILVANIA
MASSACHUSETS
NEW ENGLAND
NEW YORK
OCEAN
THE WESTERN OR ATLANTIC
The several Provinces of the English Empire in No. America are distinguished by Red, Blue, Green and Yallow according to their respective Jurisdictions. The Spanish by Brown; but the French Possessions and Encroachments are without any Colour.
The French claim all the Country within the Hudson's Bay Company's Southern Limits and the Brown Line.
The Purple Line represents the Western Boundary of the hereditary & Conquer'd Country of our Indian Friends & Allies, which has been ceded and confirm'd to us by several Treaties and Deeds of Sale.
HUDSONS BAY
NEW SOUTH WALES
LABRADOR or NEW BRITAIN
CANADA
NEW FOUND LAND
NEW ENGLAND
VIRGINIA
CAROLINA
GEORGIA
LOUISIANA
CAROLANA
FLORIDA
GULF OF MEXICO
MEXICO or NEW SPAIN
PACIFIC OCEAN OR SOUTH SEA
Bermudas
Jamaica
Antigue
Martinico
Barbadoes
Tobago

England and France competed for power in Europe as well as in the colonies. Between 1689 and 1763, the British and French fought four wars at home and abroad: King William's War (1689–1697), Queen Anne's War (1702–1713), King George's War (1740–1748) and the French and Indian War (1754–1763). Some historians call all four wars the French and Indian Wars because each pitted the British against the French and their Indian allies.

In North America, both the French and the English courted the Indians as allies, though most Indians sided with the French. Many French fur traders married Indian women. French missionaries, too, lived closely with the Native Americans. And the French showed less desire than the English to colonize Indian lands.

The English, however, won the allegiance of the five (later six) Iroquois tribes of northern New York. The Iroquois had a longstanding grudge against the French dating back to when Champlain, the founder of New France, attacked them with the first firearms they had ever seen.

Early Battles

From 1690, the governor of New France sent out parties of Canadian woodsmen and Indian allies to attack English settlements in New York and New England. One of the most famous of these raids took place in Deerfield, Massachusetts, in 1704. On a snowy night in February, a band of French Canadians and Indians slipped into the town past sleeping guards. The attackers killed settlers and burned down half the village. They took 111 captives and marched them north into Canada.

English settlers reacted to such raids by attacking French strongholds in Canada. In 1754, the English colonists captured Louisbourg, Nova Scotia. Then, in the peace negotiations, England returned Louisbourg to France, a choice bitterly resented by colonists.

The Ohio River Valley

Tensions between the French and English mounted. In 1749, a group of Virginia businessmen secured a grant from the British Crown to settle 500,000 acres of land in the Ohio River Valley. The French also claimed this land and built forts in the area to keep the British out.

The British saw this as a threat to their plans for settlement. In 1753, Virginia governor Robert Dinwiddie dispatched a twenty-one-year-old militia officer named George Washington to Fort Venango. Washington was sent to give

George Washington

George Washington made a name for himself well before he became the first president of the United States in 1789. Born on February 22, 1732, to a wealthy family in Westmoreland, Virginia, he became a land surveyor and major in the local militia by the time he was twenty years of age. The following year he trekked through snow, ice, and rushing waters to advance the interests of the British in the Ohio region. The Virginia Assembly was so impressed by Washington's report that it printed it as a small book, *The Journal of Major George Washington*. Readers agreed that Washington showed extraordinary courage and intelligence. In his fight to capture Fort Duquesne in 1755, Washington dodged four bullets that passed through his coat. This close brush with death showed Washington's courage under fire. He would go on to become commander in chief of the Revolutionary War and father of the new nation.

This French lithograph from 1854 features General George Washington (1732–1799) on horseback, fighting during the French and Indian War. The Battle of Monongahela took place in Pennsylvania on July 9, 1755. More than 1,000 British soldiers were killed during the engagement. Washington, who at the time was an aide to General Edward Braddock, managed to survive unharmed. Braddock died from his injuries four days later, on July 13, while Washington continued his military career. He eventually became a general in the American Revolutionary War (1775–1783) before serving the United States as its first president in 1789.

the French the message that the English king, George II, wanted them to leave. The French replied that they did not intend to abandon Fort Venango.

Albany Congress

In June 1754, representatives from seven English colonies and the six Iroquois tribes met in Albany, New York, to discuss a common defense against the French threat. The British government had ordered the Albany Congress to firm up the support of the Iroquois, whose traditional enemies, the Huron, were allied with the French. The Iroquois chiefs pledged their support.

At the same time, representatives of the seven colonies voted to adopt a plan suggested by Benjamin Franklin for a new union of the colonies. The colonial assemblies, however, turned down the plan. They wanted to preserve their independence.

The French and Indian War

Back in Virginia, Governor Dinwiddie dispatched a group, with Washington as lieutenant, to fortify a British fort in the Ohio River Valley. Washington and his men arrived at the site only to find the French had already taken it. Washington then found a spot for a new fort, which he named Fort Necessity, near present-day Uniontown, Pennsylvania. The French overpowered the British at Fort Necessity in July 1754.

The next battle also went badly for the British. The French defeated British and colonial troops under the command of General Edward Braddock at Fort Duquesne, near present-day Pittsburgh, in 1755. Braddock was fatally wounded. Washington took charge of the retreat out of the wilderness.

The colonists then tried to capture French strongholds in Canada. But again, they were defeated. In 1756, Native Americans raided colonial settlements in Virginia, Maryland, and Pennsylvania,

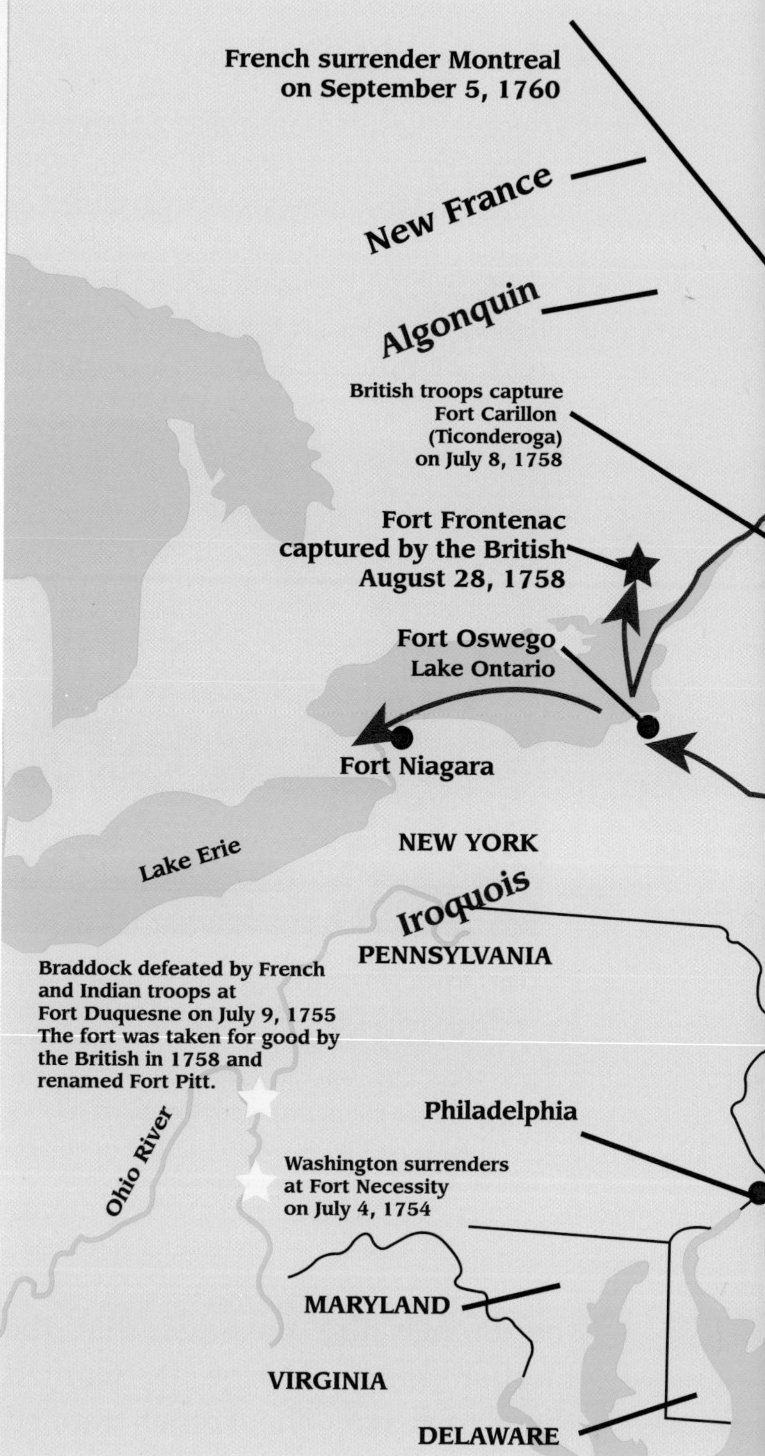
French surrender Montreal on September 5, 1760
New France
Algonquin
British troops capture Fort Carillon (Ticonderoga) on July 8, 1758
Fort Frontenac captured by the British August 28, 1758
Fort Oswego
Lake Ontario
Fort Niagara
Lake Erie
NEW YORK
Iroquois
PENNSYLVANIA
Braddock defeated by French and Indian troops at Fort Duquesne on July 9, 1755 The fort was taken for good by the British in 1758 and renamed Fort Pitt.
Ohio River
Philadelphia
Washington surrenders at Fort Necessity on July 4, 1754
MARYLAND
VIRGINIA
DELAWARE

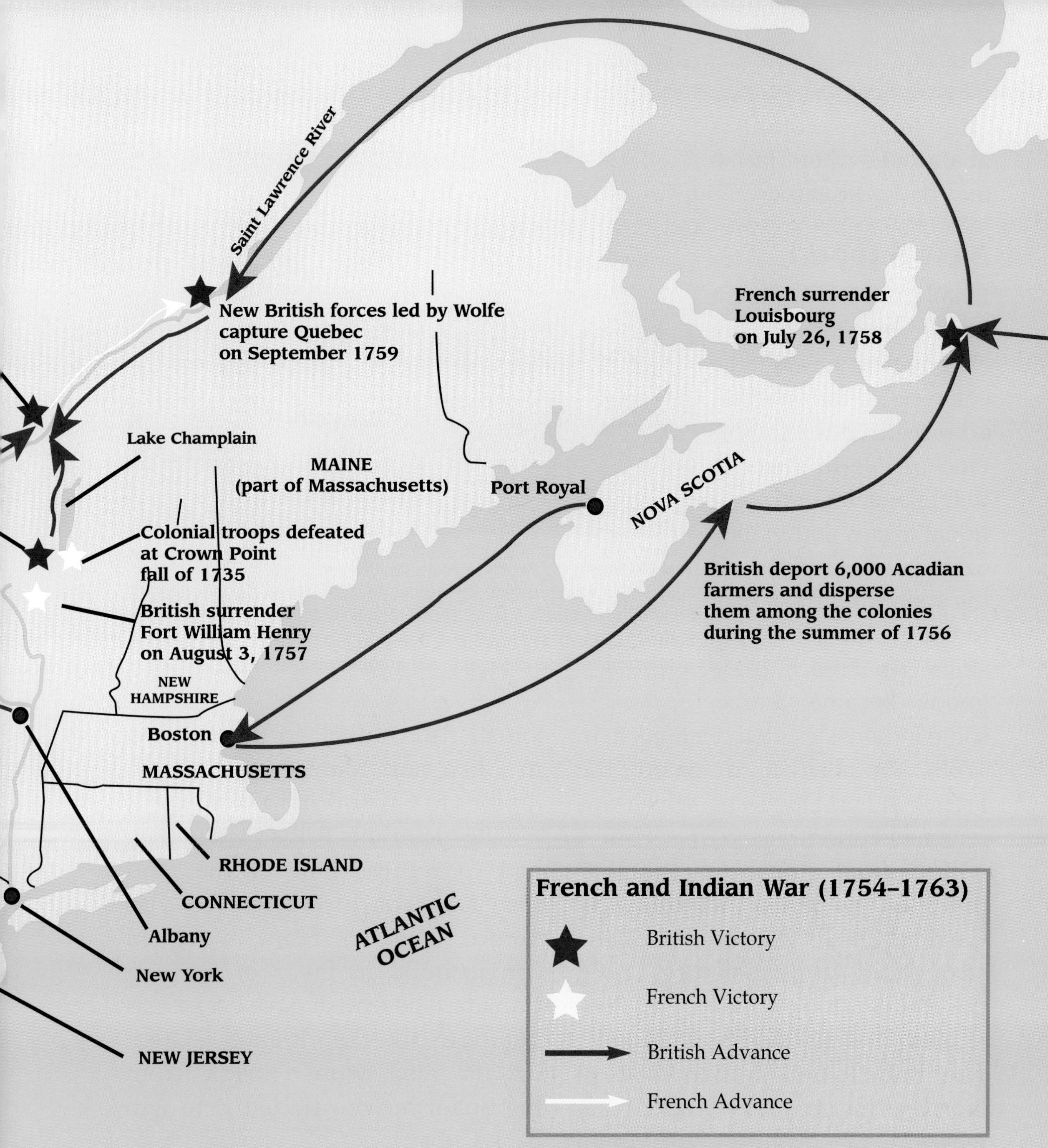

British and French advancements and victories can be seen on this map showing the major developments during the French and Indian War (1754–1763). This conflict was started because both France and Great Britain had territorial interests in dominating North America. Originally the French maintained the upper hand in the war, but soon British superiority reigned. As seen in this map, the British won important battles beginning in 1758. They were victorious in the Battles of Louisbourg, Fort Frontenac, Fort Carillon (Ticonderoga), Crown Point, Fort Duquesne (Pittsburg), and Fort Niagara.

and many colonists abandoned their farms and fled eastward.

New Support

Finally, in 1757, British prime minister William Pitt helped reverse the colonists' ill fortune. Pitt, who realized the importance of North America to England, offered additional troops and money to the colonists. Pitt used his powerful British fleet to cut off French supply ships. As French trade goods became scarce, some Indians deserted the French. In 1758, the British defeated the French at Fort Duquesne, which was renamed Fort Pitt.

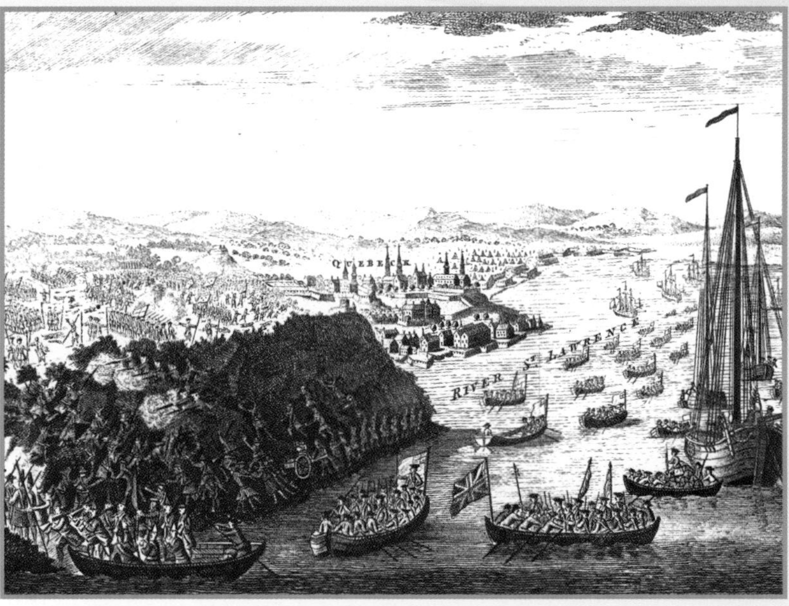

This engraving of Quebec, which renders the defeat of French forces against the British during the French and Indian War, was originally printed in *London Magazinc*. Thc Scptcmber 1759 event known as the Battle of Quebec was a decisive defeat in the conflict. It led to the fall of Montreal and, within a year, a full British victory.

The final phase of the war involved a British advance on Canada. The British recaptured the stronghold of Louisbourg. Then the British took Quebec in September 1759 and Montreal in 1760. The French and Indian War in North America was over. Elsewhere, it raged on. In 1762, Spain joined the conflict, losing Havana in Cuba and Manila in the Philippines to Great Britain.

The victorious British knew they had to return some of the land they had won to keep peace with France. Benjamin Franklin argued convincingly in favor of keeping Canada. The British gave back Guadeloupe to the French. Great Britain also won Florida from the Spanish, who traded it to win back Cuba.

CHAPTER SEVEN
The Road to Revolution

The French and Indian War changed the ways in which the French and English authorities viewed each other. In the early days of the colonies, England was too busy fighting its own civil and foreign wars to fully control the colonies. Still, as long as the colonists sent fish, furs, and other goods back to England, they were permitted to govern themselves.

During the French and Indian War, British officials came into closer contact with the colonists. They discovered that the colonists routinely ignored British trade regulations. The Navigation Acts (1651) dictated where the colonists could buy and sell their goods. Colonists, for instance, were supposed to import molasses from the British, rather than French or Spanish islands in the West Indies. Nevertheless, the colonists smuggled imported (and less expensive) molasses from the French West Indies even while England was at war with France. The colonists cared more about their own economy than about loyalty to their mother country.

The war had been costly, doubling the British debt. The English were already paying heavy taxes so they wanted the colonists to contribute to paying off the war debt. Meanwhile, the colonists viewed British troops in America as intruders. The colonists no longer needed Great Britain to protect them against Canada. Many of the settlers in America felt they could assert their independence.

Pontiac's Attack

Indians in the West heard from their French allies that the British intended to rob them of their hunting grounds. In 1763, they revolted under the leadership of Ottawa chief Pontiac and attacked colonial forts west of the Appalachian Mountains. The British were so desperate to destroy the Indians that they sent blankets infected with smallpox to the tribes.

Authorities in London came up with a plan to prevent a full-scale war with Native Americans. The Proclamation Line of 1763 set up the Appalachian Mountains as a barrier between the colonists and the Indians. British troops would help enforce the new decree.

Many colonists viewed this enforced barrier as a betrayal. The British army protected the Indians from colonists rather than allowing them to expand their settlements. Many settlers ignored the newly imposed Proclamation Line.

Sugar Act

Sugar was important to the colonists because it was used to make molasses, which, in turn, could be made into rum. New England merchants found that it was less expensive to buy molasses from the French colonies than the English colonies in the West Indies.

In 1733, the Molasses Act imposed a duty on molasses bought from French, Dutch, and Spanish islands. But the law wasn't enforced. In 1764, the British Parliament voted to replace the Molasses Act with a new Sugar Act, which would be enforced. The British authorities believed that, since colonists had regularly paid a bribe of a penny and a half to customs officers to ignore the tax, they could well afford to pay the new duty of three pence a gallon. In addition, British authorities also put higher duties on coffee and wines imported into the colonies.

Stamp Act

In March 1765, the British Parliament passed the Stamp Act on top of the duties on imported goods. A stamp needed to be applied to every piece of printed matter used in the colonies. This tax applied to newspapers, magazines, calendars, and the like. Anyone who purchased an item without a stamp on it could be fined or placed in jail.

The colonists protested angrily to what they saw as British tyranny. They boycotted (refused to buy) British goods. In October 1765, representatives from nine of the thirteen colonies met at a special congress in New York to demand

Paul Revere engraved this etching that illustrates four sides of an illuminated obelisk that was erected in Boston after the repeal of the Stamp Act in 1766. From left to right, each section depicts the phases of struggle Americans faced against the legislation. They are titled, "America in distress apprehending the total loss of liberty"; "[America] implores the aid of her patrons"; "[America] endur[e]s the conflict"; and "[America] has her liberty restored by the royal hand of [King] George the Third."

the repeal of the Sugar and Stamp Acts. The colonists believed that only their own assemblies should have the power to tax them. The motto "No taxation without representation" was born.

Because of the boycott, British sales fell dramatically. London merchants demanded that Parliament repeal the Stamp Act, which it did on March 18, 1766. At the same time, however, the lawmakers passed a Declaratory Act stating that Parliament still had the right to determine colonial law.

Benjamin Franklin, who represented the colonists in London, told Parliament that colonists opposed the Stamp Act because it was an internal tax rather than an external tax like import duties. Parliament responded by passing a series of taxes in 1767 known as the Townshend Acts. Named for British chancellor Charles Townshend, these laws requested duties on a wider range of imported items, including lead, glass, paper, paint, and tea. Eventually, most of the Townshend Acts were also repealed, but the one on tea remained.

Samuel Adams (1722–1803), cousin of U.S. president John Adams, was a graduate of Harvard University (then Harvard College) and soon became active in local Massachusetts politics. He was diligently opposed to British taxation of American colonists without their representation in Parliament. Adams is remembered as a delegate to the Continental Congress (1774–1781), a signer of the Declaration of Independence, and the governor of Massachusetts from 1794 to 1797.

Boston Massacre

Colonists resented the British troops stationed in Boston, New York, and Philadelphia. These soldiers took part-time jobs from local men. Their presence seemed like an armed occupation. In Boston, mobs of citizens taunted the British soldiers, cursing them and sometimes assaulting them. On March 5, 1770, the crowd jeered and pelted the soldiers with snowballs. The soldiers fired, immediately killing three civilians and fatally wounding two more. Samuel Adams, one of the leaders of the movement for independence, dubbed the incident the Boston Massacre.

Boston Tea Party

In 1773, Samuel Adams organized the Boston Tea Party. The rebellion began in response to Great Britain's policy of letting the British East India Company sell tea to the colonies without paying taxes. Colonists protested what they viewed as Great Britain's unfair monopoly on tea. The showdown occurred on December 16, 1773. That night, groups of Bostonians disguised as Indians boarded British ships in Boston Harbor. They opened wooden chests of tea and dumped their contents into the icy water.

The British government responded to the Boston Tea Party by cracking down on the colonists. British officials shut down Boston Harbor. They restricted self-government by requiring the governor's approval for colonial meetings.

Massachusetts put out a call to the other colonies to stop all trade with Great Britain. On September 5,

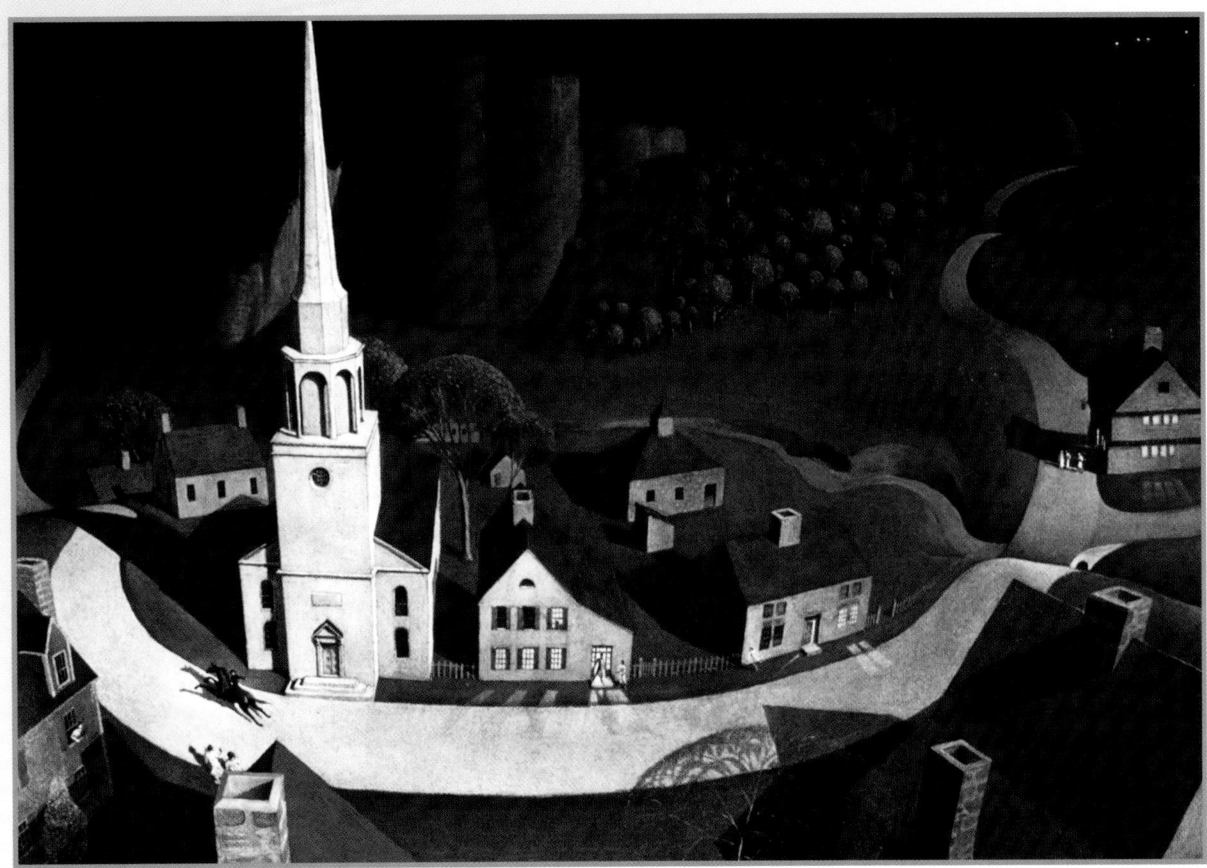

American artist Grant Wood painted this scene that depicts Paul Revere's (1735–1818) horseback ride on April 18, 1775. Revere, an enthusiastic patriot, had taken part in the Boston Tea Party. His famous midnight ride warned colonists that the British were heading toward Boston prior to the beginning of the American Revolutionary War.

1774, delegates from all the colonies except Georgia met in Philadelphia for a meeting called the Continental Congress. The Congress formed the Association of 1774, which united the colonies in their ban of British goods. Soon the Congress agreed to cease all trade with Great Britain. The delegates agreed that Parliament could not tax the colonies.

Early in 1775, war between the American colonists and Great Britain seemed unavoidable. British troops entered Boston, and the American colonists formed special groups of soldiers known as minutemen.

Before long, the first shot of the Revolutionary War was fired. At midnight, on April 18, 1775, Paul Revere set off on his famous ride warning that the British were coming.

TIMELINE

1492 Columbus makes his historic voyage to the New World.
1497 Cabot sails to Newfoundland.
1499 Vespucci explores the coast of South America.
1507 Waldseemüller names the new continent "America."
1513 Ponce de León explores Florida.
1524 Verrazano sails down the East Coast of North America.
1534 Cartier explores the Saint Lawrence River in Canada.
1539–1542 De Soto heads expedition to the American Southeast.
1540–1542 Coronado leads an expedition to the American Southwest.
1565 Spanish establish a settlement in Saint Augustine, Florida.
1565 Spanish drive French Huguenots out of Florida.
1584–1587 Raleigh sends colonists to Roanoke.
1588 England defeats the Spanish Armada.
1607 English found Jamestown, Virginia.
1608 French found Quebec, Canada.
1609 Hudson explores the Hudson River region.
1614–1618 The Married Peace between English colonists and Indians in Virginia.
1619 First Africans are brought to Jamestown, Virginia.
1620 Pilgrims settle in Plymouth, Massachusetts.
1623 Dutch buy Manhattan Island.
1630 Puritans settle Massachusetts Bay Colony.
1635–1636 Connecticut is founded by settlers from Massachusetts.
1636 Rhode Island is founded.
1660 Charles II becomes king of England.
1664 The English seize New York and Delaware.
1675–1676 King Philip's War pits English colonists against Indians.
1676 Bacon's Rebellion occurs in Virginia.
1680 Pueblo Rebellion drives Spanish out of New Mexico.
1692 Spanish recapture Santa Fe; Witchcraft trials begin in Salem, Massachusetts.
1732 Georgia is founded as a charitable colony.
1739 Slaves in South Carolina revolt in Stono Rebellion.
1754–1763 French and Indian War pits the British and colonists against the French and their Indian allies.
1763 The Treaty of Paris requires France to surrender Canada to Great Britain.
1763 Proclamation Line restricts colonists to land east of Appalachian Mountains.
1764 British Parliament passes the Sugar Act.
1765 British Parliament passes the Stamp Act.
1766 British Parliament repeals the Stamp Act but passes the Townshend Acts, which put new duties on imported goods.
1770 British soldiers open fire on civilians, an event known as the Boston Massacre.
1773 Colonists rebel against British by staging the Boston Tea Party.
1774 First Constitutional Congress meets in Philadelphia.
1775 Revolutionary War begins.

GLOSSARY

Beringia A "land bridge" of glacial ice that existed between Russia and Alaska thousands of years ago.
caravan A large covered wagon.
commission An authorization to carry out a task.
conquistador A Spanish conqueror of the New World.
democracy Government by the people exercised either directly or through elected representatives.
dissident A person who disagrees with the ruling opinions of a governor.
duty Tax on imported or exported goods.
dysentery An infection of the intestinal tract producing severe diarrhea.
enclosure System of converting common land into private property.
encomienda The Spanish system of enslaving Native Americans and making them practice Christianity.
epidemic An outbreak of a disease affecting many people.
genocide The systematic, planned destruction of a racial, political, or cultural group.
hacienda An estate in a Spanish colony.
Huguenots French Protestants.
indentured servant A person who is contracted to serve a master for a certain period.
longitude Angular distance east or west.
malaria An infectious disease characterized by cycles of chills, fever, and sweating and transmitted by the bite of an infected mosquito.
Married Peace Improvement in relations between colonists and Indians prompted by the marriage of John Rolfe and Pocahontas.
mercantilism Colonial economic policy in which the colonies benefit the mother nation; economic policy that favors exporting goods more than importing them.
mission A place where church leaders teach their beliefs.
missionary A person sent to convert others to his or her religion.
Northwest Passage A waterway that existed only in legend thought to lead from North America to Asia.
Pilgrims Puritans who settled in Plymouth, Massachusetts.
proprietary colonies Settlements owned by individuals rather than by stock companies or the Crown.
pueblo An Indian village with houses made of adobe (sun-dried mud bricks).
Puritans Protestants who wanted to purify the Church of England, originally known as English Calvinists.
Quakers Members of the Society of Friends religion.
Saint Augustine A city in northern Florida that was once an early Spanish settlement.
smallpox An acute, highly infectious viral disease characterized by high fever and pustules.
typhoid An acute, highly infectious disease caused by bacillus transmitted by contaminated food or water.

FOR MORE INFORMATION

APVA Jamestown Rediscovery
1367 Colonial Parkway
Jamestown, VA 23081
(757) 229-4997
e-mail: jamestown@apva.org
Web site: http://www.apva.org

Plimoth Plantation
137 Warren Avenue
Plymouth, MA 02360
(508) 746-1622
Web site: http://www.plimoth.org

Web Sites

Due to the changing nature of Internet links, the Rosen Publishing Group, Inc., has developed an online list of Web sites related to the subject of this book. This site is updated regularly. Please use this link to access the list:

http://www.rosenlinks.com/ushagn/coam

FOR FURTHER READING

Favor, Lesli J. *Francisco Vásquez de Coronado: Famous Journeys to the American Southwest and Colonial New Mexico.* New York: The Rosen Publishing Group, Inc., 2002.

Lukes, Bonnie L. *Colonial America* (World History Series). San Diego, CA: Lucent Books, 2000.

Masoff, Joy. *Colonial Times 1600–1700* (Chronicle of America). New York: Scholastic Inc., 2000.

Rengel, Marian. *John Cabot: The Ongoing Search for a Westward Passage to Asia.* New York: The Rosen Publishing Group, Inc., 2002.

BIBLIOGRAPHY

Blow, Michael, ed. *The American Heritage History of the Thirteen Colonies.* New York: Simon and Schuster, Inc., 1967.

Legay, Gilbert. *Atlas of Indians of North America.* Hauppauge, NY: Barron's, 1995.

Matthew, Terry. "Lecture Four: The Great Awakening." http://www.wfu.edu/~matthetl/perspectives/four.html.

Miller, Lee. *Roanoke: Solving the Mystery of the Lost Colony.* New York: Arcade Publishers, 2001.

Morley, Jacqueline. *Exploring North America.* New York: Peter Bedrick Books, 1996.

Taylor, Alan. *American Colonies: The Settling of North America.* New York: Viking Penguin, 2002.

INDEX

About the Author

Joan Axelrod-Contrada is a freelance writer and author. Her articles have appeared in the *Boston Globe* and *Writer's Digest.* This is her fourth book. She lives in western Massachusetts with her husband Fred, children Amanda and Rio, and dog Bandit.

Credits

Cover (background), pp. 16–17, 26–27 courtesy of the General Libraries, The University of Texas at Austin; cover (top right), cover (bottom left), pp. 30, 42, 51, 57 courtesy of the Library of Congress, Prints and Photographs Division; pp. 4–5, 22–23, 34–35, 40–41, 46, 48–49 courtesy of the Library of Congress, the Geography and Maps Division; pp. 8, 9, 14, 24, 29, 36, 39, 44, 54 © Hulton/Archive/Getty Images; p. 10 © Corbis; p. 11 © Bildarchiv Preussischer Kulturbesitz/Art Resource, NY; p. 18 © Nik Wheeler/Corbis; p. 19 © Bettmann/Corbis; p. 20 © George H. H. Huey/Corbis; p. 21 © Kevin Fleming/ Corbis; p. 25 © The Art Archive/Victoria and Albert Museum London/Sally Chappell; p. 31 © The New York Public Library/Art Resource, NY; pp. 32–33 © Royalty-Free/ Corbis; p. 37 © 2003 Picture History, LLC; p. 38 © Historical Picture Archive/ Corbis; p. 58 © New York Historical Society, New York, USA/The Bridgeman Art Library; p. 59 © Francis G. Mayer/Corbis.

Designer: Tahara Anderson; **Editor:** Joann Jovinelly